THE ELEMENTS OF
BUSINESS WRITING

THE ELEMENTS OF BUSINESS WRITING

Gary Blake and Robert W. Bly

New York   San Francisco   Boston
London   Toronto   Sydney   Tokyo   Singapore   Madrid
Mexico City   Munich   Paris   Cape Town   Hong Kong   Montreal

Copyright © 1991 by Gary Blake and Robert W. Bly

Library of Congress Cataloging-in-Publication Data
Blake, Gary.
 Elements of business writing / Gary Blake and Robert W. Bly
  p. cm.
 Includes index.
 ISBN 0-02-008095-6
 1. Business writing. 2. English language—Business English.
 I. Bly, Robert W. II. Title.
 HF5718.3.B53 1992 91-41283
 808'.06665—dc20   CIP

20 19 18 17 16 15 14 13

Printed in the United States of America

To my daughter, Samantha
G.B.

To my son, Alexander Thomas Bly
R.B.

Contents

3 Principles of Wording and Phrasing 35

4 Principles of Tone 55

5 Principles of Persuasion 75

6 Principles of Punctuation, Grammar, Abbreviation, Capitalization, and Spelling 93

Punctuation

7 Principles of Format 125

Acknowledgments

More than any other type of book, a book about writing is a collaboration. Countless people whose names do not appear on the cover have helped us sort out the rules, guidelines, and opinions that form this book. Others have helped us in the expression of those rules; still others have guided our words into book form.

Special thanks to Amy Bly and Eve Blake—wives, writers, and co-workers—as well as to Fern Dickey.

Thanks also to our agent, Dominick Abel, who encouraged us, and to our editor, Natalie Chapman, whose editing kept us from straying from our own principles of plain English.

A tip of the hat to our students, colleagues, clients, and teachers—the people who have helped us hone our thoughts about business writing. And a deep bow to the late E. B. White and William Strunk, Jr., whose *Elements of Style* serves as a model and an inspiration to us, as well as to everyone who struggles to write well.

Introduction

All across the United States, several million business letters, memos, reports, manuals, proposals, brochures, press
releases, and advertisements will be written today. Practically every one of them will contain writing errors.
Many of these business documents will be wordy and dis-
organized. Some will be redundant and hedgy, filled with
antiquated phrases, overblown expressions, and clichés.
Some will be poorly punctuated, poorly subordinated,
and filled with errors in grammar. Others will be vague, too
abrupt, or simply slow to get to the point at all.
Why, then, despite dozens of books already in the field,
have we written *The Elements of Business Writing*?
In our view, no one has yet written a book that weds the
simple wisdom of Strunk and White's *Elements of Style* with
writing examples taken from the world of business. Our
book uses the "before and after" format Strunk and White
used but fuses it to samples of interest to people in business,
industry, and government. The examples in this book come
from years of experience in running "Effective Business

Writing" seminars for corporations and government agencies throughout the United States and Europe.

Bad writing hangs on a long time in business because new employees tend to check through old files to see how others have written a memo or a letter before they write one. So it's no surprise that antiquated expressions and stuffy, pompous nineteenth-century verbiage emerge from twentieth-century word processors! This book aims at updating those filing cabinets by giving contemporary advice on the style, tone, and format of business writing.

The Elements of Business Writing is a concise style guide. We are able to be selective in the rules we've chosen to include, because we don't believe that every rule of writing is of equal interest to businesspeople. For example, many businesspeople trip over the comma, the hyphen, and the apostrophe—and these marks receive the most attention in the book. As for grammar, we don't inundate the reader with myriad rules, for we know from experience that most businesspeople have problems with the same five or six grammar principles, including subject-verb disagreement, run-on sentences, and dangling modifiers.

Many businesspeople still remember the horror of having an English teacher's red pen scrawl all over a composition or term paper. Some emerged from these classes hating to write, fearful that each comment in red represented an insurmountable and important writing problem. In our book, we want to present you with the chief writing issues one at a time. That way, you can begin to see them in perspective and not as a chain of problems surrounding you and stifling your unique style. By focusing on what goes wrong in writing and how to fix it, you'll view writing as a practical, problem-solving skill.

Finally, we want to provide rules, when possible, to help people understand that one person's opinion isn't always as good as another's. We want to provide authoritative advice to help writers of clear, crisp prose avoid getting caught up in the pompous and antiquated style that some corporate cultures foster among employees.

Businesspeople become demoralized when supervisors change their words and alter their styles. Maybe the supervisor has helped, rendering your work clearer or more concise. Or maybe the supervisor has actually hurt your writing by changing the style to one that hedges or is more passive. Perhaps, too, your supervisor has arbitrarily added his or her comments and neither helped nor hindered your style. Our book aims at giving you clear, consistent help. Not everything in writing is subject to rules, and we'll let you know when you're hearing our opinion rather than a generally accepted principle.

We want to guide you toward good writing, showing you exactly how it can go off track. By making our table of contents comprehensive, we hope you'll be able to pinpoint the areas you want without having to wade through irrelevant detail. Our examples are designed to give you models that epitomize a clear, conversational style. Everything in the book has one goal: to help you write better and faster. Now we're going to show you how.

1

Principles of Composition

Each businessperson develops a writing style that is the product of education, experience, and the array of on-the-job perceptions often described as the "corporate culture." As a way of fitting in, people in business often try to absorb and reproduce a writing style aimed as much at soothing managerial egos as being clear and concise.

The dramatic demand for training in business writing, however, shows that clarity and conciseness are often subverted by corporatese and institutionitis as well as by gaps in formal education. In an effort to avoid making waves, businesspeople often waffle in attempts to get to the point, summarize ideas, and make recommendations. There are several valuable principles that can help business writers express ideas in a lively, authoritative, and original way. Here are a few general rules that apply to business writing:

Rule 1. Use the active voice.

The active voice is one in which the subject performs the action:

John recommended the budget cuts.

The passive voice is one in which the subject is acted upon:

The budget cuts were recommended by John.

Using the active voice will make your writing style more direct and vigorous and your sentences more concise. Compare the relative directness of the following examples:

Passive	*Active*
It was felt that the budget was too large.	Lynn felt the budget was too large.
The findings were analyzed by Tom.	Tom analyzed the findings.
When your order is received, your desk will be sent.	When we receive your order, we will send your desk.
Fuel-cost savings were realized through the installation of thermal insulation.	The installation of thermal insulation cut fuel costs.

Some businesspeople purposely use passive language as a way to avoid responsibility or to remain anonymous. If you write, "The status of your account will be checked and confirmed," you leave it vague as to who will do the checking. But when you write, "I will check and confirm the status of your account," you are taking responsibility—which is what your reader wants you to do.

Some risk-averse businesspeople avoid the active voice because they feel it puts their heads on the chopping block. Such thinking can be dangerous, though, for passive language often suggests evasion and arouses suspicion. Active language, in contrast, reflects authoritativeness and shows you are taking charge.

The passive voice does have its place: Use it when the doer of the action is either unknown or less important than the action itself:

The company was founded in 1953.

Do you know when a decision will be reached?

The memo was sent yesterday.

The Better Business Bureau Award of Man of the Year was given to Dr. John Bonapart for his contribution to research methodology.

In this last example, the passive voice is acceptable because the person or organization doing the rewarding is less important than the person receiving the reward.

Rule 2. Avoid long sentences.

When is a long sentence too long? It's a matter of judgment, since there can be well-constructed sentences that run fifty or more words and are still easy to understand. And there are shorter sentences that seem endless because of poor construction or a profusion of technical terms.

One easy test for determining whether your sentence is too long is to read it aloud. If you run out of breath, the sentence is probably too long. But a more telling way to recognize a sentence that is too long is to read it aloud *to someone else.* If the listener gets confused or starts to forget the ideas in the early part of the sentence before you've finished reading it, the sentence probably requires breaking.

Some lengthy sentences may be helped by eliminating wordy phrases and redundancies; others can benefit from being broken into two or more smaller sentences.

Here are some examples of lengthy sentences and suggested ways of breaking them for greater clarity.

Lengthy	*Shorter Sentences*
Although in the course of product management's research it seemed as though APEX offered better and quicker service to its customers, we were informed that SMA has many of the same services available, including quick card replacement, a 1-800 hotline, greater acceptability, lower fees, and free address cards.	Although in the course of product management's research it seemed as though APEX offered better and quicker service to its customers, we were informed that SMA has many of the same services available. These services include quick card replacement, a 1-800 hotline, greater acceptability, lower fees, and free address cards.

Lengthy	*Shorter Sentences*
I suggest that we change our service and supply more fast food to give your employees what they seem to want so we can better compete with the Mendota Mall, our main source of competition in the area.	I suggest that we change our service and supply fast food to give your employees what they seem to want. That way, we can better compete with the Mendota Mall, our main source of competition in the area.
On the previous evening, July 21, the reinsured, its outside counsel for its corporate principal (Dunn, Inc.), and its corporate indemnitor (Jane Corp.) entered into a series of settlement agreements whereby the reinsured released the corporate indemnity of Jane Corp. and, in turn, all of Dunn's right title and interest in the shipyard were transferred to Woodhull Shipyard Inc.	On the previous evening, July 21, the reinsured, its outside counsel for its corporate principal (Dunn, Inc.), and its corporate indemnitor (Jane Corp.), entered into a series of settlement agreements. In these agreements, the reinsured released the corporate indemnity of Jane Corp. In turn, all of Dunn's right title and interest in the shipyard were transferred to Woodhull Shipyard Inc.

In the last example, we broke the original sentence into three shorter sentences. But we also had to add a transition ("In these agreements") to help orient the reader. Transitions help readers follow the sequence of ideas from sentence to sentence. That's why we chose to retain "In turn" as a natural bridge into the ideas of the third short sentence.

Breaking up a lengthy sentence need not involve splitting the sentence into two or three parts. When you have a "laundry list" of parallel ideas, you can often break a sentence into a series of bulleted items (see also Rule 65). For example:

The advantages of their system over ours are that theirs eliminates all CDP forms, increases productivity by 40 percent, reduces errors to near zero, and eliminates the necessity of typing customer notices and key punch sections.	The advantages of their system over ours are that theirs: • eliminates all CDP forms. • increases productivity by 40 percent. • reduces errors to near zero • eliminates the necessity of typing customer notices and key punch sections.

While breaking up lengthy sentences can add clarity, make sure you don't get carried away. Business writers who, in an attempt to avoid errors, write nothing but short sentences, can end up with a series of choppy thoughts that are dull and sound childlike. Occasionally, you need to knit two or three short sentences into a more full-blown thought. For example:

I tried to reach you by telephone. However, I was unable to do so. The reason for my call was to let you know we still haven't received your premium payment of $36.	Although I was unable to reach you by telephone, I want to let you know that we haven't received your premium payment of $36.
I went to the Conference Center on Wednesday. Soon I met the instructor. We had lunch. Then we started the class.	After going to the Conference Center on Wednesday and meeting the instructor, we had lunch and started the class.

Rule 3. Use simple language.

Some people think that using simple language means that the thinking is simplistic. They're wrong. Potent thoughts are often embodied in simple language. The point of writing is to communicate clearly. Using overly complicated words violates that basic rule and sets up barriers. Also, by dressing up your thoughts in complex language, you may exhaust your reader.

Simple language is not the province of children or uneducated adults, but of clear thinkers. Consider the following:

In reference to the situation in France, there have been certain setbacks . . .	The news from France is bad.
	—WINSTON CHURCHILL
The potential for fearing the future is actually the greatest deterrent to conquering our apprehension about the economy.	The only thing we have to fear is fear itself.
	—FRANKLIN ROOSEVELT
When it comes to your child's health, the parent can make use of his or her own inner intuition in determining a course of action.	Trust yourself. You know more than you think you do.
	—DR. BENJAMIN SPOCK
It's advisable to purchase stocks when their prices are depressed and to sell them at the top of the market.	Buy low and sell high.
	—BERNARD BARUCH

Advertising often succeeds by using simple phrases: "Don't leave home without it." "We bring good things to life." "It's finger-lickin' good." "We try harder." "When you look good, we look good." "We love to fly and it shows."

Using complex words and expressions sets up barriers between you and your reader when your job is to include your reader in your communication. So why write "aggregate" when "total" will do the job or "for the above reasons" when "for these reasons" says it simply?

Be assured that necessary steps have been taken to advise the appropriate credit bureaus of this matter.	We've informed the appropriate credit bureaus of this matter.

Should you wish to return the vehicle, please contact the undersigned.	If you want to return the car, call me.
The lack of training has a deleterious effect on our company.	Lack of training harms our company.
There is no justification for the obfuscation in the proposal.	There is no reason for the confusion in the proposal.
We are experiencing difficulties with the automatic teller machines.	We are having problems with the automatic teller machines.

The problem with today's business writing is not that it is too simple but that it blithely ignores or exhausts the reader. Experienced writers understand that even sophisticated readers like a break from polysyllabic words, long sentences, endless footnotes, and writing aimed at showing off.

Simple language doesn't mean that every term is explained at the simplest level possible but that you explain your ideas so that the least educated or knowledgeable member of your audience can easily understand what you are saying and in fact cannot misunderstand you.

Is it necessary to keep things simple even when addressing internal audiences, people who understand our jargon and big words? Does a scientist writing to a scientist have to use simple language? Can you get too simple? If you write a journal article so that the layman can grasp it, will the article offend technicians? Will it be ten times longer than necessary because you define everything for the lay reader?

Decide these questions by asking yourself, Who is my reader? and Who else is likely to read what I've written? Temper the principles presented in this book with your special knowledge of the unique audience you are addressing. Let yourself be guided by your readers' particular needs in any given situation. Write to the level of your audience. If you are writing for an audience that includes both scientists and laypersons, make your material understandable to the latter. If your audience consists of scientists exclusively, write your material so that it is clear to the least informed in your subject area.

Rule 4. Delete words, sentences, and phrases that do not add to your meaning.

Unlike free-lance writers, who are used to writing within prescribed word lengths, business writers rarely restrain the urge to go on and on. In an attempt to force his subordinates to be concise, former president Ronald Reagan, while governor of California, refused to read memos that ran longer than a single page.

Writers who waste words waste their readers' time. Instead of "in the majority of instances," write "usually"; rather than "at this point in time," write "now."

Your reader's time is precious. If you take three pages to communicate what you could in a few paragraphs, your reader may not bother to finish what you've written or may skim it with impatience and miss some important points. Most people already have enough reading material piled up in their "in" boxes. Don't add to the flood. Cut all unnecessary words from your writing.

Of course, it is possible to write a ten-page memo that's concise; length is often determined by content. But for some forms of business writing (a résumé, for instance) there is an "ideal" length—one page. Most letters and many memos rarely need to exceed that length. Reports may run from one to ten pages, and most proposals, even complex government ones, needn't exceed 100 pages.

Use the fewest words possible to communicate your meaning. Don't clog your memos, letters, and reports with unnecessary words.

Here are several examples of wordy sentences and possible revisions:

Wordy	*Concise*
A check in the amount of $1,000 is being sent to you.	I'm sending you a check for $1,000.
We understand that you recently wrote us to ask about your Keogh account.	You recently wrote us to ask about your Keogh account.
It has come to our attention that your account is two months in arrears.	Your account is two months in arrears.
The offer is an unusual one and will not be repeated.	This unusual offer will not be repeated.
The designer shows a preference for track lighting.	The designer prefers track lighting.
Please file away this letter.	Please file this letter.
Let's not prolong the duration of this meeting.	Let's not prolong this meeting.

Becoming sensitive to verbosity requires you to develop the habit of reading over the first draft of anything you write with a sharp eye for the flab. If you spot constructions that take too long to make the point, try shorter ones.

In Chapter 3, we provide a list of common wordy and redundant phrases. Study the list and then watch for similar words and phrases in your own writing; edit out anything that can go without damaging your message.

Some phrases commonly used in business and government are so weak or flabby that instead of substituting for them you can omit them from anything you write:

the fact that
it has been shown that
it is recognized that
it has been demonstrated that
it must be remembered that
it may be seen that
what is known as

it is worthy of note
it will be appreciated that
it is found that
it may be mentioned that
it is the intention of this writer to
deemed it necessary to

Rule 5. Break your writing into short sections.

A general principle of good writing is to divide the subject into topics and cover each topic in a paragraph. A further principle of good business writing is to make each paragraph relatively short.

Using a paragraph to cover a topic serves to guide the reader through the development of your ideas; each new paragraph signals that a new topic has been reached.

Short paragraphs are easier to read. Readers rebel against large chunks of type. They absorb information more easily when it is presented in short, coherent units.

If possible, break long paragraphs—those of ten lines or more—into smaller ones. The division should occur the moment one topic ends and a new one begins. But be careful: Make sure that the first sentence beginning a new paragraph isn't actually more appropriate as a final sentence that completes or rounds out the topic of the previous paragraph.

Here's a long paragraph that could be broken into two shorter ones:

LENGTHY PARAGRAPH

In our telephone conversation on June 13, 1990, you informed me of the error in my letter of April 11 in which I neglected to include the total of all premiums paid into your policy account. I am very sorry for this error and for any confusion it may have caused you. Fortunately, our files contain accurate totals. Our records show that you have paid a total of $8,000 into the annuity and $24,000 into your policy account. As you know, all of your annuity premiums and accumulations have been transferred to the policy account, and you are currently receiving them as income under your policy account #33221.

BETTER

In our telephone conversation on June 13, 1990, you informed me of the error in my letter of April 11 in which I neglected to include the total of all premiums paid into your policy account. I am very sorry for this error and for any confusion it may have caused you.

Fortunately, our files contain accurate totals. Our records show that you have paid a total of $8,000 into the annuity and $24,000 into your policy account. As you know, all of your annuity premiums and accumulations have been transferred to the policy account, and you are currently receiving them as income under your policy account #33221.

Breaking a long paragraph into two smaller ones will not, of course, solve matters of wordiness or poor organization. At best, it signals a new topic and allows a reader to mentally take a breath between weighty chunks of thought.

Rule 6. Use specific and concrete terms.

"If those who have studied the art of writing are in accord on any one point," write Strunk and White in *The Elements of Style*, "it is on this: the surest way to arouse and hold the attention of the reader is by being specific, definite, and concrete. The greatest writers—Homer, Dante, Shakespeare—are effective largely because they deal in particulars and report the details that matter."

Specific, concrete terms paint a vivid picture in your reader's mind. Vagueness makes the picture blurry. Businesspeople sometimes use vague terms out of laziness; often they become intentionally vague to gloss over a matter or buy "wiggle room."

For example, take "finalize," a term the business world has adopted. Although it sounds definite, it leaves its exact meaning unclear. If a client says that our contract will be finalized next week, what does that mean? That it will be signed? That there will be agreement to sign it? That a written draft will be prepared? It's anyone's guess.

Here are some other vague expressions, followed by more specific ways of wording the idea:

Please let me know your comments and concerns so that we can make the data as complete as possible.	Please make sure this ad has all the information we discussed on the phone.
Does cross-selling have a positive impact?	Does cross-selling increase revenues?
This will give us enough time to reach some meaningful conclusions.	This will give us enough time to determine our budget.
As requested, I called several brokers who had not been notified.	At Tom's request, I called four brokers who had not been notified.
Send it to me ASAP.	If possible, please send it to me by Monday.

Generalities may be convenient to use and come easily to mind, but they force the reader to work to figure out your exact meaning. If, for example, you ask a colleague how the recent staff meeting went, you might be told, "Fine." If you probe further, you might learn that "we accomplished a lot." If you dig for specifics, perhaps you'll find out what you wanted to know in the first place: "We decided to hire three new typists, buy four personal computers, and revamp our vendor file." Say exactly what you mean, and don't force your reader to probe for specifics or second-guess your meaning.

Rule 7. Write in a natural, conversational style.

Don't use words inside a business office that would sound unnatural outside it. Good writing should sound like conversation.

"If you were speaking to a customer," writes John DiGaetani in the *Wall Street Journal*, "would you ever say:

'Enclosed please find your order for three (3) replacement keys'? If you did, your customer would surely think you were weird."

Apply the conversational test to rid your writing of stilted wording, a prissy tone, stiff and formal phrasing, and jargon that can obscure your meaning and alienate your readers.

Here are some examples of unconversational businessese, followed by a more natural way of expressing each thought:

If further information is required, you may contact Barbara Sue Covello.	If you'd like more information, please call Barbara Sue Covello.
Your earliest attention to the above matter is absolutely imperative.	Please send us your check by Friday.
Upon receipt of your check, further attention will be given to your request.	When we receive your check, we'll begin work on your request.
He has stated that Margery Gross and myself have been a great help to her.	He said that Margery Gross and I have been a great help to her.
Prior to this announcement, we ascertained the parties affected.	Before this announcement, we found out whom it would affect.
Pursuant to our discussion, I am forwarding the book.	As we discussed, I'm sending you the book.

Writing conversationally is not a mandate for using slang or colloquialisms. Just as business writers must avoid lawyerlike, formalistic phrases, they must also eschew the chummy tone of colloquialisms. Slang and colloquial language may work on certain speaking occasions, but they are rarely appropriate for any but the most informal business communications—not only because such language sets an inappropriate (often negative or inadvertently offensive) tone but also because it quickly becomes cliché or can be misunderstood:

Let's not drag this out.	Let's do this as quickly as possible.
Keep your shirt on.	Please be patient.
I could care less.	I couldn't care less.
It's asinine to blow our chances by being late.	It's foolish to lose the account by being late.
Mark's been canned.	Mark's been fired.
It's fourth down and goal to go.	This is our last opportunity to make the sale.
Break a leg!	Good luck!

Rule 8. Keep ideas parallel.

Ideas that parallel one another in content should parallel one another in form. According to *The Elements of Style*, "The likeness of form enables the reader to recognize more readily the likeness of content and function."

"One if by land, two if by sea."

"Where there's a will, there's a way."

"I came, I saw, I conquered."

"Saw sub, sank same."

"Ask not what your country can do for you, ask what you can do for your country."

There are various categories of parallelism. The sentences above show parallel construction within a sentence, but the principle of parallelism can also apply to the wording of a list of items or to the structure of a series of elements within a sentence.

Parallel construction clarifies meaning, creates symmetry, and lends equality to each idea in the series. In fact, the previous sentence is an example of parallelism. Note that each of the three elements of the sentence contains a verb-noun combination: "clarifies meaning" . . . "creates symmetry" . . . "lends equality . . . " A violation of this principle might have been "parallel construction clarifies meaning, creates symmetry, and each idea has a sense of equality."

Please complete this form, sign it, and then it should be sent to me.	Please complete this form, sign it, and send it to me.
Now is the time not for caution but courage.	Now is the time not for caution but for courage.
It was both a long meeting and very disorganized.	The meeting was long and very disorganized.

Present lists of items in parallel form:

The guide includes:	The guide includes:
• passport requirements	• passport requirements
• city maps	• city maps
• what to wear and pack	• advice on what to wear
• when to go	• suggestions on when to go
• a list of restaurants	• a list of restaurants

In the list on the left, three of the items begin with a noun; two *(what, when)* do not. In the list on the right, each item begins with a noun.

In the right-hand list below, each item starts with a verb:

At the meeting, Mr. Heyward	At the meeting, Mr. Heyward
• reported on the budget	• reported on the budget
• was asked a question about training, and he answered it	• answered a question about training
• explained the new filing system.	• explained the new filing system.

Parallelism requires that an article or preposition applying to items in a series be used either with the first item only or with each item; it should not be applied inconsistently.

The manufacturing, the accounting, advertising, sales, and IS departments

The manufacturing, the accounting, the advertising, the sales, and the IS departments

Typewriter ribbons may be stored in the desk, parts room, or in the cabinet.

Typewriter ribbons may be stored in the desk, parts room, or cabinet.

2

Principles of Organization

Most business documents serve one of two basic purposes: They either inform or persuade. This chapter shows how to organize business documents that *inform*, such as memos, letters, and business reports. (Chapter 4 deals with how to organize persuasive documents, such as sales letters and proposals.)

How important is it to organize your writing sensibly and logically? At least as important as style, tone, word choice, and grammar. If your readers believe the information is important to them, they may read your report even if it's poorly written. But if it's poorly organized, they won't.

How you organize your material—that is, choosing what goes first, second, third, and so on—determines, to a large extent, whether you effectively communicate your main points to your readers. Here are a few basic principles for organizing business writing:

Rule 9. Organize your material according to the way your reader thinks about the subject.

Most businesspeople are busy and will not read documents that do not hold their attention. To gain and keep your readers' attention, you'll need to put what they want to hear above what you want to say. This means (1) starting with what's important to them, not what's important to you, (2) organizing the material like a newspaper article—in order of most important to least important, and (3) knowing the way your reader thinks about the subject. All of this also means, of course, knowing your audience.

How do you organize your writing according to the way your reader thinks about the subject? By putting yourself in the reader's shoes and asking, What about this subject concerns my readers most and would gain their interest?

Consider what you would do if assigned to write an overview of your corporation. If you were aiming the presentation primarily at new employees, you might start with a history of the company, present an overall corporate philosophy or mission statement, then discuss the various divisions or subsidiaries and the role or purpose of each. Within each division, you would cover the major products and the market for each.

On the other hand, if the primary audience was investors, you would begin with an overview of the current year's sales and financial performance, compare it with previous years to show growth and progress, then break down sales and contributions to the bottom line by division or product line.

Creating an outline can help you organize your material so that it's reader oriented. The simplest type of outline is the one you learned in school: major headings and subheadings are set off using Roman numerals, capital letters, Arabic numerals, and lowercase letters. For example:

Marketing Plan for Liftex Corporation

I. Overview
   A. Company background
   B. Product line
   C. Customer profile

II. Markets
   A. Pulp and paper industry
   B. Chemical-process industry
   C. Food processing

III. Marketing Strategies
   A. Data base marketing
      1. Size of data base
      2. Design of data base
      3. Sorts and selections
      4. Summary of current data base marketing activities
      5. New data base marketing programs
         a. monthly mailings
         b. special offers and discounts
         c. quarterly customer newsletter
   B. Direct mail
      1. Generic mailings
      2. Industry-specific mailings
      3. Product-specific mailings
   C. Print advertising
      1. Media schedule
      2. New ads planned
   D. Public relations
      1. Article placement
      2. Press releases
      3. Speeches
      4. Presentation of technical papers at major conferences

IV. Budget

V. Action Plan
  A. Budget
  B. Schedule
  C. Responsibilities

To create your outline, you might write your key points on index cards, then group the cards according to major subject categories; these major subjects become the Roman numerals I, II, III, and so on of your outline.

Another outlining technique, proposed by Gordon Burgett in his book *Empire-Building by Writing and Speaking,* is to organize your informational document as a "working question" (the main point phrased as a question) supported by a group of "secondary questions" (the who, what, when, where, why, and how).

For example, if you are writing a report explaining to others in your company the benefit of working with your department, the main point, phrased as a working question, might be How can I benefit from the services of department X? Now sit down and make a list of all the questions your readers are likely to ask about working with department X. These become the secondary questions. The outline for this report, including secondary questions, appears below:

Working question:
How can I benefit from the services of department X?
Secondary questions:
What is department X?
What does department X do?
What services do they provide to support other groups within the corporation?
How can I gain maximum benefit from these services?
Should I use department X or hire an outside vendor?
How is my group billed for department X's services?
How do I go about initiating a project with department X?

The main advantage of this approach is that it helps organize the information in your document according to the way your reader would think about the topic, not according to your interests or viewpoint. A disadvantage is that it forces the reader to read (or at least skim) your entire document to get the gist of the story. This can be avoided by using an executive summary at the beginning (see Rule 12).

Rule 10. Organize your material logically.

If you are unsure as to how your reader thinks about the subject, choose an organizational structure that logically fits the material.

In some situations you may not know what he or she wants to read about first. Maybe you aren't familiar with the audience you'll be writing for and can't get good information about it.

Or perhaps you must write a single document appealing to multiple audiences—and so you can't really make the piece as reader-specific as you'd like.

How, then, do you organize your writing? In general, it's best to stick with standard formats. A laboratory report, for example, has an abstract, a table of contents, a summary, an introduction, a main body (theory, apparatus and procedures, results, and discussions), conclusions and recommendations, nomenclature, references, and appendices.

A business plan might include these sections: executive summary, company overview, description of the product or service, market analysis, marketing and sales plans, funds required and funding uses, financial data, and appendices.

Some other common formats include the following:

- *Order of location.* An article on the planets of the solar system might begin with Mercury, the planet closest to the sun, and end with Pluto, the planet farthest away. If you're writing a memo on the status of the company's plants, you might organize it by state or region.

- *Alphabetical order.* A logical way to arrange a vitamin catalog (A, B, B₁, and so on) or a directory of company employees is alphabetically.

- *Chronological order.* This format presents the facts in the order in which they happened. History books are written this way. So are many case histories, feature stories, annual reports, corporate biographies, and minutes of major meetings.

- *Problem/solution.* Another format appropriate to case histories and many types of reports is the problem/solution format, which begins with "Here's what the problem was" and ends with "Here's how we solved it, and here are the results we achieved."

- *Inverted pyramid.* This is the newspaper style of news reporting in which the lead paragraph summarizes the story, giving the reader the *who, what, when, where, why,* and *how;* the paragraphs following present the key facts in order of decreasing importance. You can use this format in journal articles, company newsletters, press releases, memos, letters, and reports.

- *Deductive order.* Start with a generalization—a theme you want to support or a point you want to make—then support it with as many facts and observations as possible. Scientists use this format in research papers that begin with the main thesis or finding and then state the supporting evidence. Sales managers and copywriters use it in preparing persuasive sales letters. This organizational scheme works well when you are writing to promote a preconceived notion or idea and you need to gain the support of others by presenting facts and logical reasons why your proposition makes sense.

- *Inductive order.* Begin with specific instances and examples and then lead the reader to the idea or general principle the evidence supports or suggests. An excellent way to write articles for the trade press.

- *List.* Simply list in one-two-three fashion the key points you want to cover. A memo to your boss might be entitled "Ten Recommendations on Immediately Reducing the Operating Expenses of the Composite Materials Research Program" if your boss told you her main concern was budget overruns. A bulletin sent to customers might bear the headline "Seven Ways to Use Your Ajax Widget-Washer More Effectively."

- *Priority sequence.* Rank recommendations, problems, concerns, issues, or other items from the most important to the least important—an ideal format for writing a letter or memo recommending a series of steps or actions.

Rule 11. Delete the warm-up paragraph.

A "warm-up paragraph" is an opening paragraph that does not add to your meaning but serves as a lead-in to the main body of your work. Usually it can be profitably removed without destroying the basic structure of the piece.

Frequently, the warm-up paragraph presents background material that, while relevant, does not contain the main news or item of interest and therefore is unessential.

Are we saying you shouldn't present background information? No. If it's valuable, it should probably come early in the report or memo. But don't lead with it or you'll lose your reader. Your first paragraph should engage the reader by arousing curiosity or presenting important news in a clear, compelling fashion.

Warm-up paragraphs appear in print when writers allow their first draft to stand as the final draft or fail to revise with a critical eye. If they aren't sure how to get started when they start writing, they may fumble along for a few sentences until they feel comfortable.

This may be a good way to overcome writer's block, but it usually results in opening sentences that lack sharpness and fail to gain attention or generate interest.

Some warm-up paragraphs can be deleted altogether; others should be revised or moved. Here's the opening paragraph from an article published in a leading engineering journal:

> It is both exciting and rewarding to discover that the scientific principles of one's profession can have immediate and gratifying expression in daily life. A case in point occurred recently, and I think it is appropriate to relate.

This paragraph, presumably written to ease the reader into the article, does not contain news, important facts, or items of interest. It goes without saying that the writer "think[s] it is appropriate to relate"; otherwise, why would he write the article in the first place? The opening would be stronger and arouse greater interest if the author had deleted the unnecessary paragraph and plunged right into the story!

Here's a sample of a first paragraph in a business memo written by someone who didn't first clarify why she was writing and what she was trying to communicate:

> The above subject was raised at a meeting on October 4 between our respective departments regarding transfer and rehire processing. It was agreed that we would investigate a method of retaining a transfer employee record if the transfer was within the profit centers. The input routine is currently designed . . .

What's the news? There isn't any. The author's recommendations, which were the result of two months' work, were buried in the middle of the second page of the memo. Her boss very likely missed them. (Also, note now the heavy use of the passive voice deadens the language and gets between the material and the reader's understanding —see Rule 1.)

If she'd identified her ideas before sitting down to write the memo, she might have started like this:

> After researching a way to keep old employee transfer records, I propose that we (1) remove three unnecessary codes that take up valuable disk space and (2) change the codes on transfer

employees. This will avoid confusion, make it easier to gain access to old records, and reduce data entry time and effort.

The above paragraph is specific, presents benefits, and says what the boss really wants to know. In informal memos or letters, warm-up paragraphs can sometimes help orient the reader, but the amount of "warm-up" copy should be kept to a minimum; the sooner you get to the point, the better:

I enjoyed meeting you last Thursday. Shirley was wonderful, and your entire staff radiated enthusiasm for the marketing project. I know that Tom and his team can handle the job. I have assembled and enclosed the documents that address your request for information as it concerns this project. . . .	I enjoyed meeting you and your staff last Thursday. Here's the information you asked for concerning the marketing project we discussed.

Rule 12. Use an executive summary.

An executive summary is a short paragraph or section that precedes the main document. It's similar to the abstract of a technical paper in that it summarizes the major points of a lengthy document in a few short sentences or paragraphs.

You need an executive summary when your document becomes so long that you think many of its intended readers won't read it or when the text is so detailed that your main points seem buried and don't come across forcefully. The executive summary is designed for those who don't have the time or inclination to read the full text.

For a one- or two-page letter or memo, an executive summary isn't needed. But it may be desirable for a longer proposal, report, or manual. In the defense industry, where proposals can run into thousands of pages and are typically presented in multiple volumes, a short executive summary of only a few pages will usually precede the main proposal. In a lengthy memo, the executive summary need not be given a separate heading; the first paragraph can serve as a summary:

> At your request, and under our Contract C-995, we tested 1,200 of the used parts and components from the inventory you purchased from UniTech. We found that 1,116 of them—93 percent of the test sample—were in acceptable working condition.

Or the first paragraph can be used to introduce the material to come:

> At the request of Mike Mutsakis, I am writing you to clarify the understanding that American Widget Co. had regarding relocation expenses for Peter Addison.

Similarly, the executive summary of a lengthier document, such as a report, can also be used to list the findings or serve as an introduction and orientation to the material to come.

> This report presents a list of the missing tapes in the video library and recommends ways to replace them. Specifically:
>
> - There are 174 tapes missing, of which 140 are lost or stolen and 34 are misplaced or not returned by borrowers.
> - We should write off the permanently lost or stolen tapes and purchase replacement copies for 90 of them at a cost of $1,800.
> - We should track down the misplaced tapes through the sign-out records.
> - We should restrict access to tapes in the future and suspend the borrowing privileges of patrons who fail to return tapes on time.

Another example:

> In response to the charge of discrimination against Wilson, Smith & Sons, we deny any discrimination against Etta Jones,

the charging party, on the basis of her age, race, or color. Following is information concerning Etta's employment with our company, our position regarding the allegations against us, and our response to your request for a statement on our position concerning her pending lawsuit.

To get a feel for how to write executive summaries, read course descriptions in college catalogs. These write-ups are essentially executive summaries of the more detailed course outlines handed out during the first class.

Rule 13. Separate fact from opinion.

Good business writing separates fact from opinion. Unlike polemic, dogma, and rhetoric, business writing is meant to clarify rather than confuse, to present a point of view supported by reason rather than force an idea or concept upon a reader.

Why is it important to separate fact from opinion in your business writing? Your readers will make business decisions based on the information contained in your document, so they need a means of assessing the accuracy and reliability of each statement.

For instance, if you say, "The XL-100 pump is rated to handle pressures ranging up to 450 psi," the reader whose application produces 400 psi (pounds per square inch) can feel confident about specifying your pump. But if your reply to their query about pressure is "I feel pretty confident our pump can handle your pressure requirements," that's probably not good enough. And since choosing the wrong pump could result in equipment damage, explosions, or loss of life and limb, you must be clear about what is fact and what is opinion.

To separate fact from opinion, business writers must be able to recognize each. In some cases, it's clear-cut; in others, it's not.

When you say that Babe Ruth hit sixty home runs in 1927, you're stating a fact. There's no reason to phrase it as an opinion; the writer who writes, "I think it was Babe Ruth who hit sixty home runs in 1927" has not done an adequate job, because the statistics can be looked up and confirmed.

When you say, "I think interest rates will drop to 9 percent by the end of the year," that's an opinion. No matter how knowledgeable you are in economics, predicting interest rates is more guesswork than science, and no one can know for certain whether they will rise or fall.

How do you separate fact from opinion? One simple technique is to divide your document into sections with headings that indicate whether each section contains facts or opinions.

A business report, for example, might contain the following sections: *executive summary, background, findings, conclusions,* and *recommendations.* The background and findings contain the facts; conclusions and recommendations are your opinions formed as a result of your consideration of the facts. When you break the document into sections, your readers can more easily determine when you're presenting facts and when you're giving an opinion.

Another way to indicate an opinion is to preface your statement with the phrase "In my opinion." But be selective about using it and similar phrases. Depending on the circumstances, the audience, and the writer, it can serve either to confirm accuracy or to avoid responsibility.

Take the sentence "In my opinion, the Macintosh is the best personal computer for Ajax Company's office use." If you're a computer consultant hired by a company to help them select the right microcomputer for their office, using the phrase "In my opinion" sidesteps your responsibility and weakens your recommendation. After all, you're the expert; you should be able to assert authoritatively which is the best computer for the client's application—and why.

On the other hand, if you're a secretary and you're asked to try both an IBM and a Macintosh and then give your opinion as to which you like best, using "In my opinion" acknowledges that you're not a computer expert and are simply voicing a personal preference.

At times, you'll legitimately use "In my opinion" and similar phrases to distinguish what is fact and what is opinion. But keep in mind that knowledgeable people write authoritatively. Good writers try to push the "I think" into the "This is true."

I think our billing software is ready for beta testing.	Our billing software is ready for beta testing.
In my opinion, she is the best person for the job.	She is the best person for the job.
Perhaps the cafeteria manager should take some cooking lessons.	The cafeteria manager should take some cooking lessons.

The use of superlatives *(best, leading, easiest, state-of-the-art, superior)* unsupported by facts signals to the reader that you are expressing an opinion rather than stating a fact. Good writers replace superlatives with specifics to make sentences more factual and therefore more persuasive.

The Honda Accord is the best compact car on the market today.	The Honda Accord is the most popular compact car on the market today.
The NetCom data network's performance to date has been virtually error-free.	The NetCom data network's performance to date has been 99.98 percent error-free.

Rule 14. Delete unnecessary closings.

Strong documents are often ruined by weak closings. The reason: The writer, not knowing the most appropriate way to close, founders around for a few paragraphs, saying essentially the same thing in three or four different ways to make sure the reader gets the message.

Decide how you want to close, say it once, then get out. If

you want to meet with the reader, say, "I'd like to get together with you to discuss this situation in more detail. I'll call in a few days to arrange a meeting." If you are writing to a subordinate, you might say,"Let's meet in my office at 9:00 A.M. on the twelfth to discuss this. Please call me to confirm."

What closings are weak? "Thanking you in advance" is one. It's presumptuous: It assumes your readers have accepted your offer before they've actually agreed to it. "Thanking you in advance" is frequently used when the writer knows he or she has failed to make a persuasive argument and hopes the readers will comply anyway, simply because they've been thanked.

"If you have any questions, please call" is also overused. It often masks the writer's *real* request, which is for a meeting, a signature, a go-ahead, funding, a check, an order, a contract, or whatever. If you want a signed contract, say, "Please sign the enclosed contract and return one copy to me," not, "If you have any questions, please call." Rest assured, if your readers have questions, they'll call or write before doing anything else.

"Don't hesitate to call" is a cliché. It conjures up an absurd image of the reader hunkered over his or her desk, one hand hovering uncertainly over the telephone, reaching and pulling back, then reaching and pulling back again, hesitating to call.

When suggesting a meeting, do not add the phrase "at a time and date convenient to you." If you're dealing with a superior, peer, prospect, or customer, your reader will understand that he or she has the right to select the time and date. When writing to a subordinate, suggest the time and date.

"I look forward to working with you" is acceptable but too general. It is far better to state the precise nature of the work involved: "I look forward to working with you on improving the performance of your inside sales force" is preferable because it's specific.

Be direct and original in your closings. Don't fall back on habits, clichés, or stock phrases lifted from some book of form letters. Most are antiquated, have lost their original sharpness, and serve to dull the reader interest you've worked so hard to build.

Rule 15. Use headings and subheadings.

In any document longer than one page, use headings and subheadings to guide your reader through the material. Headings and subheads serve several purposes:

- They break up the text into short sections, which makes your material easier to digest and easier to read.

- They provide quick reference points to help the reader find specific information or ideas. An employee benefits manual, for example, will have separate sections on major medical, dental, long-term disability, and hospitalization coverage for easy reference.

- They enable your reader to locate key points without reading the entire document. If subheads are sufficiently descriptive of the contents of each section, the reader can get the gist of your document by scanning and reading the subheads in sequence.

Each section of your document separated by a heading or subhead should cover a single key concept or major thought. When you're ready to discuss another topic, write a new subhead and start a new section.

Subheads for business documents can be terse and to the point or longer and more descriptive. It depends on the document and your personal style.

In a report, for example, each subhead might be the name of a major section—executive summary, background, findings, conclusions, recommendations.

Other documents might have more descriptive heads and subheads. A computer manual, for example, might contain subheads like these:

Turning on Your Desktop System
Setting up a Data Base
Maintaining Your Files
Adding or Deleting Names in the Data Base
Creating Personalized Letters

Although brevity in heads and subheads is a virtue, don't be *too* terse or you'll risk losing in clarity what you gain in conciseness. Our recommendation is that you use subheads or headings that are more descriptive, even if it means increasing the length.

System Overview	How Staff Attorneys Can Benefit from Using the New LAWNET Data Base
Accounting Reports	1991 Versus 1990 Annual Revenues
Business Plan	A Proposed Schedule for Opening Three New Branch Offices in Chicago, Los Angeles, and Toronto

Whenever possible, keep subheads in a document parallel:

Opening a Document File
Creating a Data Base
Revising Data Base Entries
Exporting Files to Other Programs
Consulting the System Dictionary
Checking for Errors and Inconsistencies

For most typewritten business documents, use a major heading for the document followed by subheads for each section. Using more than two or three levels of headings (heads and subheads) is difficult to present graphically in standard typewritten material.

Underlining, capitalizing, centering, and indenting are the basic tools available on standard typewriters and word processors for graphically separating heads and subheads from the rest of the text. Boldfacing, available on some word processing systems, is another effective technique for adding visual emphasis to heads and subheads.

Writers who use desktop publishing systems or whose material will be typeset have a great variety of graphics available to them and can choose various levels of heads, subheads, and sub-subheads using different typefaces, weights, sizes, and styles. The key is to be consistent in the use of such graphics.

To achieve consistency, you first must determine how many levels of heads and subheads will be used throughout your document. The easiest scheme to follow is to use headings for each major section and subheads within each section. For example:

ABC System Manual

Installation Procedures
   Uncrating the System
   Inspecting Your Components
   Assembling the Components
   Testing the Assembled System

Operations Procedures
   Operating System
   Word Processing
   Data Base Management
   Communications
   Graphics
   Desktop Publishing

Maintenance Procedures
   Keyboard
   CRT
   Disk Drives

After determining how many levels of headings and subheads you will use, you must decide how you will distinguish graphically between a major heading, a subhead, and sub-subheads (if you use them).

Typically, the use of boldface type, underlining, centering, all capital letters, and larger type adds prominence to a heading. Using both uppercase and lowercase letters and not underlining or boldfacing give less importance to the heading.

3

Principles of Wording and Phrasing

The principles of good wording and phrasing are designed to make your writing direct, clear, simple, explicit, and to the point. Such a goal may sound obvious, but it flies in the face of an unfortunate tradition of pompous, jargon-ridden, sexist language, antiquated and wordy phrases, and redundancy in business writing.

This chapter outlines principles intended to strengthen and clarify business writing, to modernize style and usage, and to make it possible for your readers to grasp your meaning quickly and without ambiguity.

Rule 16. Avoid wordy and redundant phrases.

WORDINESS

Such expressions as "in the majority of instances," "at this point in time," and "after the conclusion of" use more words than necessary to convey a thought. They muddy your writing, obscure your point, and waste your reader's time.

Here are some wordy phrases and alternatives:

Wordy	*Concise*
There is no existing system that can do this.	No system can do this.
May we ask that you return her contract by Monday?	Please return her contract by Monday.
The rules are provided in the manual.	The rules are in the manual.
I'd like to apologize for any inconvenience.	I apologize for any inconvenience.
I would think that we should hold the seminar in May.	We should hold the seminar in May.
We need something along the lines of a traffic manager.	We need a traffic manager.

Here are several other common wordy expressions followed by suggested substitutions:

as you may or may not know	as you may know
at all times	always
at this point in time	now
can be in a position to	can
inasmuch as	since
in compliance with your request	at your request
in regard to	regarding
in the event that	if
in the very near future	soon
make a recommendation that	recommend
of a confidential nature	confidential
perform an analysis of	analyze
start off	start

REDUNDANCY

Expressions such as "free gift," "plan ahead," "consensus of opinion," and "foreign imports" are also wordy. Each says the same things twice: all gifts are free; "plan" implies planning ahead; "consensus" already implies an agreement of opinion; "imports," by definition, are foreign. The needless repetition of words to convey a meaning is called redundancy.

In each phrase below, one of the words tags along for the ride and should be cut loose. Take "cancel out." Cancel already contains the idea of "out," so you have a redundancy. Besides, you can't cancel "in." Or "adding together": "Adding" mean adding things together. You can't "add" apart.

Here are some of the most common redundancies:

Redundancy	*Substitution*
absolutely perfect	perfect
actual experience	experience
advance plan	plan
an asset on the plus side	an asset
an honor and a privilege	an honor
any and all	any
as a general rule	as a rule
basic essentials	basics (or essentials)
chemotherapy treatment	chemotherapy
close proximity	near
combine into one	combine
consecutive in a row	consecutive
continue on	continue
current status	status
different varieties	varieties
equally as well	as well as
ERA amendment	ERA

Redundancy	*Substitution*
estimate about	estimate
final outcome	outcome
first and foremost	first
first introduction	introduction
first priority	priority
foreign imports	imports
goals and objectives	goals
group meeting	meeting
honest truth	truth
isolated by himself	isolated
joined together	joined
necessary requisite	requisite
new breakthrough	breakthrough
one and the same	the same
overall plan	plan
past history	history
personal opinion	opinion
point in time	time
potential fire hazard	fire hazard
RAM memory	RAM
range all the way from	range from
refer back to	refer to
repeat again	repeat
small in size	small
this particular instance	this instance
true facts	facts
tuition fees	tuition
whether or not	whether
write away for	write for

Rule 17. Use small words.

Generally, good writers prefer small words to complex or elegant ones, but you'd never know that by reading business correspondence. Businesspeople like to trot out the twenty-dollar words; maybe it's because they feel those words will impress people.

Notwithstanding Scholastic Aptitude Tests (SATs) that rate our ability to define sophisticated vocabulary like "prolix" or "obsequious," the business world is better served by writers who pare down their language, who keep things simple.

To write simply is to value the communication of ideas over the need to impress others. Ask yourself: Are you trying to impress or express? The best way to impress people is not to trot out big words but to put mighty thoughts into simple, everyday words. Sam Goldwyn, the Hollywood producer known for his malapropisms, once said: "Include me out!" The job of business writers is to build a bridge to the reader, not to send him or her running to the dictionary.

In Rule 3, we urged you to cut through lofty expressions in an attempt to be clear and straightforward; in this rule, we urge you to prefer the smaller word to the larger word when both say essentially the same thing.

Here are some sentences using big words, followed by sentences that say the same thing—but better—with smaller words:

We will order all the materials on this list you furnished.	We will order all the materials on the list you sent.
The aggregate of the three proposals amounts to $3,890.	The total cost of the three proposals is $3,890.
This is the optimum solution.	This is the best solution.
We need to maximize profits in 1991.	We need to increase profits in 1991.

Here are some big words to avoid (and their substitutes):

Big Word	*Small Word*
abbreviate	shorten
aggregate	total, whole
amorphous	shapeless
ascertain	find out
assist	help
beverage	drink
commencement	start
conceptualize	conceive, think of
concept	idea
conjecture	guess
currently	now
deficit	shortage
demonstrate	show
duplicate	copy
expedite	hasten, speed
facilitate	ease, help
feasible	possible
finalize	complete, finish
furnish	provide, send, give
indicate	tell, say, show
maintenance	upkeep
obtain	get
optimum	best
parameters	boundaries, factors
prioritize	order
receive	get
terminate	end
utilize	use
viable	workable

Rule 18. Avoid sexist language.

Over the past twenty-five years, the world of business has grown sensitive to the problem of sexist terms. Increasing numbers of books and magazine articles have focused attention on sexism in all forms. Now that women make up more than half the work force, it is no longer accurate—or fair—to use terms that once were taken for granted. We can't assume anymore that a mail carrier is necessarily a "mailman" or that the person who chairs a meeting is a "chairman."

Nor is it accurate to use a term like "workmen's compensation" when those compensated include women and when there's a simple alternative: "workers' compensation."

By calling certain words and phrases "sexist," we are not endorsing a political or social philosophy so much as urging businesspeople to acknowledge the changing business climate. In the past, one might assume male dominance in an occupation. No longer. Using language that does not restrict itself solely to the male gender is good business because it is realistic, recognizes the current shifts in the work force, and avoids alienating women.

Effective business writers strive to rid their work of both overly sexist words and inadvertent sexist references. Here is a list of common sexist terms followed by suggested substitutes:

ad man	advertising executive
anchorman	anchor
chairman	chair, chairperson
cleaning woman	domestic, housekeeper
coed	student
draftsman	drafter
Englishmen	the English
fireman	firefighter
foreman	supervisor
housewife	homemaker
maiden name	birth name, former name

to man (verb)	to staff, run, operate
man-hours	work-hours, person-hours
mankind	humanity, humankind
my girl	my secretary
newsman	reporter, journalist
policeman	police officer
poetess	poet
postman, mailman	mail carrier
repairman	service technician
salesman	salesperson
self-made man	self-made person
spokesman	spokesperson
stewardess	flight attendant
the working man	the wage earner
weatherman	weathercaster, meteorologist
workman	worker

Inadvertent sexist references arise out of assumptions that certain jobs are occupied only by males. For instance:

Typically, a manager with DCD Corp. will call a meeting with his staff.

It is assumed in this sentence that the "manager" is male.
There are several ways you can rewrite your way out of this problem. First, you can eliminate the pronoun:

Typically, a manager with DCD Corp. will call a staff meeting.

Second, you can recast a sentence into the plural:

Each employee must decide for himself.	Employees must decide for themselves.

Third, you can replace the sexist term with the second person "you." This works when you are giving instructions to readers:

| All salesmen must sell two cases. | You must sell two cases. |

Fourth, you can alternate male and female examples. This can give equality to a piece of writing in which examples ("John Doe enters his code name on the computer") tend to be predominantly male, thus giving a skewed vision of the role of women in a department or organization. Give "Jane Doe" equal time.

Finally, you can substitute "he or she" for the traditional, old-fashioned "he" when the antecedent's gender is unknown:

> A systems analyst must make sure that he or she does not overload the system.

This is a clumsy construction, however, and you should use it sparingly.

The avoidance of sexist terms can go too far and lead to awkward, unnatural terms. Some words are part of our common heritage and have particular value that is lost or made absurd when you try to find a substitute: craftsmanship, freshman, ombudsman (craftspersonship? freshperson? ombudsperson?).

Language is fluid, and the controversy rages on. If the sound of some of the substitutes for sexist terms is strange to your ears, remember: thirty years ago, they laughed at "Ms." Today Ms. is almost universally accepted as the correct way to address a woman. But it is only in the past few years that the *New York Times* has allowed its writers to write "Ms. Gloria Steinem of *Ms.* magazine," instead of "Miss Gloria Steinem of *Ms.* magazine."

Rule 19. Know the proper use of the most commonly misused words and phrases.

There are a number of English words that business writers commonly misuse. Some misused words sound like—or are spelled like—other words. Many, like "hopefully," are errors that gain popularity through widespread use. And still others are nonwords; that is, they are on-the-spot creations that are repeated and adopted by others.

Here are some of the words and phrases that are perpetual problems:

ability, capacity	*Ability* means the state of being able or the power to do something. (A computer has the ability to create graphics.) *Capacity* is the power of receiving or containing. (The computer has the capacity to hold 5 plug-in boards.)
about, approximately	*About* is inexact; it indicates a rough estimate. (We are about halfway there.) *Approximately* implies accuracy. (There are approximately 1.06 quarts in a liter.)
accept, except	*Accept* means to receive willingly, to agree with. (I accept your apology.) *Except* means excluding. (You'll be reimbursed for everything except local travel.)
advise, inform	*Advise* means to offer counsel and suggestions. (I advise you to buy a municipal bond.) *Inform* means to communicate information. (I inform you that your proposal hasn't arrived.)
affect, effect	*Affect* is a verb meaning to change or influence. *Effect* is a verb meaning to bring

about. *Effect* is also a noun meaning result or outcome. (The report will have the desired effect.)

aggravate

Aggravate means to make worse. Don't use it as a synonym for *irritate, annoy,* or *provoke.* (The layoffs will only aggravate the problem.)

alternate, alternative

Alternate means a substitute. An *alternative* is a choice between two or more possibilities.

anxious, eager

Use *anxious* when anxiety or worry is involved, not as a synonym for eager. (I'm anxious about my performance appraisal.) *Eager* means highly desirous of something. (I'm eager to know the results of our work.)

because of, due to

Because of means by reason of or on account of. (The conference was delayed because of snow.) *Due to* means attributable to. (Her promotion was due to her managerial style.)

beside, besides

Beside means at the side of. *Besides* means in addition to.

can, may

Can implies ability; *may* implies permission.

capital, capitol

A *capital* is a city that is the official seat of government in a political entity. *Capital* can also refer to a capital letter or to money (e.g., capital needed to start a business). A *capitol* is a building in which a legislature assembles.

continual, continuous

Continual means recurring frequently. *Continuous* means without interruption.

comprise

Comprise means encompass or include. The United States comprises (not "is comprised of") the fifty individual states.

convince, persuade

Convince means to cause someone to believe something. (The defect rate convinces me that improved quality controls are necessary.) *Persuade* means to cause someone to do something. (The recruiter persuaded me to rewrite my résumé.)

data, datum

When *data* is used synonymously with facts, it is plural. When it is used synonymously with information, it is singular. The singular form *datum* has fallen out of popular use.

disinterested, uninterested, bored

Disinterested means impartial. *Uninterested* means indifferent. *Bored* means tired by dullness or repetition.

e.g., i.e.

e.g. means for example; *i.e.* means in other words, or that is.

farther, further	*Farther* refers to physical distance. (He is farther away from the plant than he is from headquarters.) *Further* means "to a greater degree or extent" and refers to matters in which physical measurement is impossible. (Further research would be helpful.)
fewer, less	*Fewer* is used when units or individuals can be counted (fewer memos). *Less* is used with quantities of mass, bulk, or volume (less space).
finalize	Use *complete* or a more specific term. Not: "We are going to finalize your contract." Instead: "We are going to sign your contract."
hopefully	*Hopefully* means in a hopeful manner or filled with hope. The phrase "hopefully the situation will improve" makes no sense because the situation cannot be filled with hope. "Hopefully we shall fly to Pittsburgh tomorrow" does not mean we hope to fly to Pittsburgh tomorrow; it means we shall fly there filled with hope. Beware of *hopefully*.
impact	Do not use *impact* as a verb meaning to affect or influence. To *impact* means to drive or press closely into

	something (an impacted tooth). If you want to say X had an impact on Y, say X *affected, influenced,* or *impinged on* Y.
irregardless	Not a word. Use *regardless.*
like, as	*Like* means "similar to." It is still not acceptable as a conjunction. It is acceptable, however, when it introduces a noun not followed by a verb. (This coffee is like an espresso.) *As* means in the same way or manner. (Think as I think.)
over, more than	*Over* implies position. Do not write *over* when you mean *more than.* (There are more than two hundred branches nationwide.)
percent, percentage	*Percent* means per hundred. (The account earns 10 percent interest.) *Percentage* means a proportion or share in relation to a whole. (His company has a small percentage of the total market.)
practicable, practical	*Practicable* means that which appears to be feasible. *Practical* is an adjective used to indicate that a thing or activity is useful.
presently, at present	*Presently* means soon; *at present* means now.
principle, principal	*Principal* used as a noun means head of a school, a main participant, a sum of

money. As an adjective, it means first or highest in rank, worth, or importance. A *principle* is a fundamental law, a basic truth.

prioritize

Prefer *make priorities* or *order.*

should, will

Should implies ought to, a belief. *Will* is a prediction.

strategize

Awkward. Use *make strategies.*

that, which

Ideally, *that* is used with a restrictive clause—a clause absolutely necessary to the meaning of the sentence. (This is the project that will launch your career.)

Which is used with a nonrestrictive clause—a clause that is parenthetic and is not necessary to the meaning of the sentence. (The executive committee, which is made up of vice-presidents, has not discussed the problem.)

ultimate, penultimate

Ultimate means last. *Penultimate* means next to last. Do not use penultimate as a superlative of *ultimate.*

unique

No superlatives are needed, since *unique* means one of a kind. Therefore, *really* unique, *so* unique, *most* unique, and similar constructions are grammatically incorrect.

| who, whom | Use *who* as a substitute for *he, she,* or *they.* (Who will be the boss—Bill or Sheila?) Use *whom* as a substitute for *him, her,* or *them.* (To whom shall I bill the room charge—him or her?) |

Rule 20. Substitute modern business language for antiquated phrases.

Business writing is often filled with overly formal, antiquated, and stiff phrases like "Enclosed please find," "As per your request," and "Pursuant to our conversation." Such usage is a holdover from times gone by and does not belong in contemporary business writing.

Many businesspeople like to "pump up" their writing with antiquated phrases because they feel such language adds a veneer of professionalism. But the job of writing is to express, not impress.

Business writers should strive to use modern substitutes for words and phrases that have gone out-of-date. Of course, it's natural for a new employee to look through the files to gain quick guidance in the accepted writing style of a place of employment. But beware: Those letters, memos, and reports in the filing cabinet may themselves be holdovers from many years ago. No wonder we perpetuate words and phrases that sound more in line with nineteenth-century prose than with modern-day business writing.

Often the difference is apparent when you say the written phrase out loud. Try saying this, for instance: "With kindest regards, I remain, Jane Doe." As a rule, the conversational test will help you identify language that needs modernization.

Antiquated	Modern
Kindly send us the results.	Please send us the results.
I'm not in a position to recommend you.	I cannot recommend you.
We deem it advisable for you to wait.	We suggest you wait.
I am sending you the book under separate cover.	I am sending you the book separately.
This will acknowledge your recent letter.	Thank you for your recent letter.
We are holding a two-day seminar in lieu of a one-day seminar.	We are holding a two-day seminar instead of a one-day seminar.
We are effective by virtue of our experience.	We are effective because of our experience.

Rule 21. Substitute original language for clichés.

Clichés are expressions that are used so often they lose much of their original freshness and power. For example, "user-friendly," although a relatively recent phrase, has been so widely adopted that the expression has already become a cliché.

People adopt clichés because they're familiar and handy—so handy that they're used reflexively. But the very popularity of the cliché turns it into a kind of white noise; it ceases to communicate with the same force it had when first used.

There are thousands of clichés to watch out for. Be on particular guard against the following words and phrases used all too often in business writing:

acid test
back to square one
ballpark figure/estimate
beyond the shadow of a doubt
bottom line

brainstorm
bread-and-butter issue
bury the hatchet
cost-effective
dealing with
dialogue
dos and don'ts
escalate
expertise
feedback
few and far between
first and foremost
grind to a halt
hands on
hence
heretofore
hit the nail on the head
interface with
last but not least
meaningful
meet your needs
point in time
relevant
run it up the flagpole
state of the art
take the ball and run with it
thus
under review
viable
vitally important

Rule 22. Avoid jargon.

Every industry has its "buzz words." They may be understood by everyone in the industry—airline controllers, furriers, lawyers, bankers, or automotive engineers, for example. But when insiders use such words in com-

munication with anyone not in their field, confusion
sets it.

Unlike legitimate technical terms, which even outsiders
could, if they wished, look up in a dictionary, jargon is a
private language that has meaning only to a particular
group. To air traffic controllers, "caca" and "lala" are short
for collision alert and low-altitude alert. Travel agents talk
about the "OAG" *(Official Airlines Guide).*

A business executive may know the meaning of software
and hardware but not understand terms like operating systems, applications package, or subroutine. And even an experienced programmer may be baffled by a brochure that
refers to interprocess message buffers or four-byte integer
data types.

If you are sending a memo or report to people who may
not understand the special words and phrases of your pro-
fession, find other words or else be prepared to define the
jargon you do use.

bespoke suit	tailor-made suit
deplane	get off the plane
The doctor completed the operation skin to skin.	The doctor did the complete operation herself.
functionality	functions, features
in-service	provide on-the-job training
interface (noun)	contact
interface (verb)	talk with
needs assessment	assessment of an organization's needs
one twenty	two-hour program
pub date	publication date
Third Avenue is out of our hospital's catchment area.	Third Avenue is outside the area from which our hospital can admit patients.

| Your account is domiciled at this branch. | Your account is at this branch. |

It's acceptable to use a technical term if you believe that at least 90 percent of your readers will understand it. But don't use jargon unless it precisely communicates your meaning and will not confuse your readers.

4

Principles of Tone

Achieving the correct tone is a subtle but important part of good business writing. Tone conveys attitude, and the manner in which you "talk on paper" to your readers has a lot to do with how they receive, understand, and respond to your message.

Tone also communicates a definite image or mental picture of you and your company to your readers. Write like a bureaucrat and your readers will think you're a stuffed shirt. Write like a concerned, helpful, friendly business professional and that's how they will see you and treat you.

Your sales bulletins, memos, letters, and proposals are like "company representatives on paper." Even interoffice memos speak volumes about you, your personality, and your style of management. Unfortunately, here's what a typical internal corporate communication sounds like:

Please find attached a copy of a news release entitled "ABC Plastic to Feature Its Extrusion and Injection Molding Products at the NPE and ANTEC Shows." This news release highlights the output extruder screw, and it is my understanding that this extruder screw is no longer a viable end product and should no longer be promoted. This release, to date, has generated three letter inquiries to the Kansas City office and, if indeed we no longer offer this product, will cause difficulties with potential customers. Will you please advise me at your earliest convenience of the correct status of this product?

Sincerely,

Pat Jones, advertising manager

Customers, colleagues, and clients like to deal with people who are warm, friendly, and pleasant. But the writer of this memo comes across as a petty martinet, falling back on such antiquated phrases as "Please find attached" (instead of the more conversational "I've enclosed" or "Here is"), "please advise" (should be "let me know"), and "at your earliest convenience" (substitute "as soon as you can").

If the writer had obeyed our "Rule 7. Write in a natural, conversational style," he or she might have written the following:

Here's a press release featuring our output extruder screw. Didn't we stop making these? If so, we shouldn't be sending out press releases promoting them. Please let me know the status of this product as soon as possible.

Sincerely,

Pat Jones, advertising manager

P.S. We've received three inquiries from this release. Should I send them our extruder screw brochure or our general all-line catalog?

One reason business and technical professionals write dense, complex, stuffy prose is to boost their own egos and make themselves feel important. For example, one of the strongest complaints businesspeople have about data processing professionals is their use of technical language. "The fact is, however, that deep down, DPers [data processing professionals] have always loved this distinction," writes Naomi Karten in *Business Computing* magazine. "They have always believed what they did was much too complicated for the 'average' person to understand." And so they use jargon, corporatese, and densely written prose to protect their superior status within the firm.

Unfortunately, this kind of mind-set produces language like the following:

> Well-designed documentation is a necessary requisite for an optimized human-machine interface.

What the writer really means, of course, is

> If we want people to be able to use the system, we need a manual that's easy to understand.

Many business writers are caught in a dilemma. They want to write more conversationally, but their supervisors tell them to write in more formal corporate language. This chapter is written to help resolve such issues and find the right tone for each document.

Rule 23. Write to express, not to impress.

Which "style" is current and correct? The trend in business writing today is to write naturally and conversationally. Modern business prose tries to capture the smooth, easy flow of conversation while eliminating the repetition, stumbling phrases (ums and ahs), and unnecessary connectives ("So I said," "You see," etc.) common to the spoken word.

Achieving this style is largely a matter of adjusting your attitude. Instead of writing to impress the reader with your importance, position, technical knowledge, or mastery of big words and fancy phrases, write to convey your meaning. This means avoiding jargon; using simple, plain language; being concise; editing carefully; and keeping your writing clear and uncomplicated. Above all, it means not using big words when a smaller one will do just as well.

"Guard against the tendency to want to write 'fancy' or 'high class,' " says Joe Vitale in *Zen and the Art of Writing*.

Many writers, especially beginners, feel they have to impress people with their knowledge of big words and complicated sentences. Don't do it. This isn't you. It's some distorted image of what you may think a "writer" [or "businessperson"] should be. Write simply, and your style will rise and flow from within you.

Whenever you write a sentence that sounds as if you're trying to impress the reader with your knowledge, position, or importance, stop. Reread the sentence. Extract the key idea you're trying to get across. Then write the thought in plain, simple English. Some examples:

The corporation has deemed it necessary to terminate the employment of Joseph Smith.	Joe Smith was fired.
In reply to your letter of August 10, please be informed that this office does not keep statistical data on the number of people in domestic employment, but it is suggested that you inquire at the Department of Labor.	We don't keep the employment records you need. Please try the Department of Labor.
To effect any change in telephone instrumentation or lines, a memorandum of justification should be submitted by the respective program telephone liaison or office manager to the supervisor of building management and planning.	To add a phone line or make any other changes in your phone system, send your request to the supervisor of building management.

Rule 24. Prefer informal to formal language.

You should write in a tone appropriate to the audience and the occasion. An after-dinner speech at the Elk's Club banquet, for example, will differ in tone from a press release announcing that your company is going into Chapter 11. But as a rule your writing should remain relaxed, friendly, and informal.

Many businesspeople—especially senior management, government employees, administrators, scientists, engineers, and technical professionals—mistakenly believe they must adopt a cold, remote, or superior tone to sound "professional" in their writing. Too bad! Boring, stiff, pompous prose has consigned thousands of letters, memos, articles, reports, and brochures to the trash basket.

When you write in an overly formal style, you sound like a lawyer or a bureaucrat. The problem is, people would rather deal with a friendly, helpful human being than a lawyer, a bureaucrat, or a cold, impersonal corporation or institution. Your writing must project a personality that is inviting to the reader, not one that turns your reader off.

When deciding on what tone to take, *err on the side of being too informal and conversational rather than too formal.* No one has ever complained that a simply written letter or report was too easy to read.

A comprehensive review of your school-based substance abuse program will be conducted by a team of field auditors from our department next week.	We'll be reviewing your substance abuse program next week.
Cell lysis (cell death) occurs when a mature virus is released from the infected cell.	When the infected cell releases a mature virus, the cell dies.

All of the bonds in the above-described account having been heretofore disposed of, we are this day terminating same. We accordingly enclose herein a check in the amount of $30,320.11, same being your share realized therein, as per statement attached.	We've sold all the bonds and closed your account. Here's a check for the $30,320.11 we owe you.

Rule 25. Prefer positive words to negative words.

In business writing, prefer positive words and phrases. Negative words and phrases, often written in anger or out of ignorance, contain implicit criticism of the reader and are frequently interpreted as arrogant or accusatory. Here are some negative phrases to avoid:

you claim	says to the reader, "You say so, but I don't believe you"
failed to	harsh and insulting; implies incompetence
neglected to	implies willful misconduct
lack of	communicates personal criticism

If you want to motivate your readers and not merely scold or punish, positive language works best. Your goal should be not to criticize, chastise, or make the reader feel guilty but to address unpleasant matters without offending and to initiate actions that will improve the situation.

This notice is regarding your failure to remit payment on our invoice.	Did you get our bill?
Mr. Lazelle claims he was never notified of the policy cancellation.	Mr. Lazelle says he was never notified of the policy cancellation.

You consistently fail to show up for work on time.	You need to improve your punctuality and get in by 8:30 A.M., as every employee is required to do.
The pricing scheme you suggested for the student version of the product is impractical.	If we can increase the profit margin by 20 percent, the pricing you suggested could work.
We're 50 percent short of our fund-raising goal.	We're 50 percent of the way toward achieving our fund-raising goal.

When you want to express a thought in a positive manner, use *when* instead of *if.*

If your performance is satisfactory, we'll end the trial period and offer you a full-time position.	When your performance is satisfactory, we'll end the trial period and offer you a full-time position.

Rule 26. In a sentence containing both good and bad news, give the bad news first.

When you want to emphasize something, put it at the end of the sentence. To be positive, a sentence should present the bad news first, followed by the good news. For example: "Although we don't have a position for you, I'm sending your résumé to someone who has a job opening in your field."

Often the bad- and good-news portions of the sentence or paragraph are separated by *but.*

Version 1.0 of the software is still selling briskly and getting rave reviews, but version 2.0 won't be ready for another six months.	Version 2.0 of the software won't be ready for another six months, but version 1.0 is still selling briskly and getting rave reviews.

We can have the brochures ready in time for the Business Expo. But because of the client's slowness in reviewing the copy, we won't be able to meet the original publication date.	Because of the client's slowness in reviewing the copy, we won't be able to meet the original publication date. However, we can still have the brochures ready in time for the Business Expo.
I'd be happy to donate the door prizes for Education Day; however, I don't have time to serve on the committee.	I don't have time to serve on the Education Day Committee; however, I'd be happy to donate all the door prizes.

Notice the difference between the two versions in the above example. In the first version, the writer ruins any positive impression donating door prizes might have made by adding a negative comment about not having time to participate more fully, and the overall message ends up being negative. The writer of the second version comes across as magnanimous: Even though she cannot be involved in the event, she cares enough to help out with a generous donation.

Rule 27. Write to change behavior, not to express anger.

A letter written in anger should never be mailed. Instead, put the letter in a drawer overnight and take a look at it again the next morning. The twenty-four hours between first draft and second look give your anger a chance to dissipate, enabling you to produce a letter that's constructive rather than damning.

Write to achieve the desired action or thought on the part of the reader, not to vent your own feelings. How do you change behavior or thought or persuade the reader to see your point of view? Chapter 5 gives extensive guidelines on persuasive writing; here are a few additional suggestions:

Remember that the other person doesn't have to be wrong

for you to be right. Most people are overly critical and too eager to show others they're wrong. But the other person doesn't have to be wrong for you to be right. It's far more effective to communicate that both points of view have merit, then gently suggest why your course of action is preferable.

Using Jensen Graphics is a bad idea and won't work because they don't have desktop publishing and can't make changes quickly. Martin Unlimited is the only possible choice because they have extensive desktop publishing capability in-house.

Jensen Graphics always does good work and would probably do an acceptable job designing this proposal. However, have you considered using Martin Unlimited? Their work is also excellent—and they can make changes quickly and at less cost because they have extensive desktop publishing capability in-house.

The consultant you hired is an idiot, and her "management leadership" concept is total baloney. These expensive so-called gurus are really full of hot air and charge us an outrageous fee to lecture about things that are either total common sense or else don't relate at all to our business. Therefore, I'm canceling any further training of my staff.

Talking with my staff after the first round of training sessions, I find that they haven't bought into the consultant's management concepts. Therefore, I don't feel further sessions would be beneficial—unless you or the consultant can suggest a way to overcome the resistance of our trainees. (Frankly, my managers feel the consultant's program is not practical and does not reflect adequate knowledge of the particular issues in our industry. Any thoughts on that?)

Just because your client demands a one-week turnaround after sitting on the preliminary draft for a month doesn't mean it can be done. I have many other projects on my schedule and never agreed to such a rush turnaround, which you will see if you check our original contract. Therefore, I must deny your request and will proceed with the work according to our original time line of fifteen days.

As we discussed previously, it normally takes fifteen days to generate a final report after approval of the preliminary draft. Naturally, I want to help you keep the client happy and am glad to accommodate rush requests. However, I am also concerned about compromising the quality of the work and would like to see if we can get a small deadline extension. Even a few more days would make a big difference. How about if I hand it in to you next Thursday instead of Monday?

People are more likely to follow your recommendations willingly when you allow them to do so with their egos intact.

Phrase criticism in the most positive manner possible. There are two ways to say something: the nice way and the nasty way. If you feel rushed and irritated when writing, it's easy to be careless with the tone you take in your prose. As a result, insults and abuse can creep into your writing and turn off readers when you don't really mean to.

Whenever you are forced to write something unpleasant or negative, something the reader is not likely to enjoy reading, take pains to phrase it in the most positive, constructive, and friendly manner possible.

The quality of the slides I received from you this morning is totally unacceptable.

The quality of the slides I received from you this morning is not up to your usual fine standards. But I know you can fix it easily.

The cafeteria food stinks.	We have received a number of employee complaints concerning some items on the lunch menu. I would like to meet with you to discuss some alternative choices. In particular, employees say they would like more salads and fresh foods and less meat and fried foods.
He is consistently late and seems incapable of coming in on time.	Tom's a good worker, but his showing up late is demoralizing to the other employees in the department.

Say what you liked as well as what you didn't like. When you tell someone, "I don't like [the report, presentation, drawings, plans, proposal, copy, design, or whatever]," without mentioning anything you *did* like, it ruffles feathers, damages relationships, and leaves the impression—usually inaccurate—that the work under question is totally without merit.

But is there really *nothing* you liked about the work? In most cases, your dissatisfaction is with particular portions of the whole. Much of the work may be perfectly acceptable, and pointing out the parts you liked while criticizing only those that need improvement makes your complaints more palatable and inspires a greater effort toward improvement on the part of your reader.

The quality of the slides I received from you this morning is totally unacceptable.	The quality of the slides I received from you this morning is not up to your usual fine standards. The charts and graphs look super, as always. But the word slides are blurry, and some are unreadable.

This report stinks.	There are many good points to this report: The recommendations make sense, and the conclusions are well drawn. However, the research data needs to be clearer and easier to follow.
I hated the speaker.	The speaker gave a good presentation, and many people said so. My reason for not wanting him at the national sales meeting is that I don't care for this motivational type of presentation and would rather have as our keynote speaker a recognized authority in sales training.

Suggest the course of action. To change behavior, it's not enough to criticize or point out what was wrong; you also have to tell the reader what to do to make things right.

The quality of the slides I received from you this morning is totally unacceptable.	The quality of the slides I received from you this morning is not up to your usual fine standards. In particular, the type in the word slides should be made larger, and the background should be a darker color—preferably black.
I don't like your choice of speaker.	Your speaker is certainly well known and a great orator. However, I feel that for the national sales meeting's keynote address we should

| | have Dick Jones or some other nationally recognized authority in effective sellingtechniques. |
| The annual report is boring. | The graphics are great, but I feel the copy could be stronger. For instance, one of the most exciting developments of the year was the introduction of our TC-800 line, yet this wasn't even mentioned. I think it's worth at least a page. |

Rule 28. Be your most pleasant self.

If you are always pleasant and considerate, then let your personality shine through in your writing.

Most of us, however, have our ups and downs. Sometimes we're in a good mood; at other times, we're short-tempered and irritable.

In your writing, you need to be at your best. Don't be sarcastic or high-handed. People respond negatively to others who are sarcastic, rude, arrogant, superior, or brusque. They respond much better when you are polite and courteous. So be warm and helpful.

Strive for a friendly tone. For instance, while brevity is a virtue, being too terse can make you sound arrogant or impatient.

| I have received a copy of the minutes of your October 25 meeting, and I am totally confused. Please reconsider or clarify. | Thanks for sending me the minutes of your October 25 meeting. I've looked through them, and while they contain a number of good ideas, I have some questions. For example . . . |

Have them on my desk by 8:00 A.M. Thursday.	I'd like to have them on my desk by 8:00 A.M. Thursday. Can you do it?
There will be a meeting in my office on this topic at 2:00 P.M. today.	Let's meet in my office at 2:00 P.M. to discuss this in more detail. Please let me know if that's inconvenient for you; otherwise, I'll assume you're coming.

Be courteous without overdoing it. Be direct and to the point. Don't gush or go on and on.

I'm delighted you've joined us as a member of the ARJ Referral Real Estate Network and am glad to have this opportunity to meet you on paper. You have made a wise decision coming on board our growing organization of 2,000 members in the tristate area alone, and I'm sure we'll be exchanging lots of profitable referrals in the coming months. Again, congratulations on a smart move joining ARJ. You'll be glad you did!	Welcome as a member of the ARJ Referral Real Estate Network. Your membership kit is enclosed.
Thanks for taking five minutes from your busy schedule.	Thanks for your time.

Words and phrases that can help you achieve a more pleasant tone in your writing include the old stand-bys *please, thank you, thanks, I'm grateful,* and *I appreciate.* Also helpful are *regards* (instead of sincerely) and *Would you . . . ?* (instead of a direct order).

Your writing will also sound more pleasant when you use personal pronouns (I, we, you) instead of the third person (they, the company, the client, the customer, the prospect).

Worthington strives to provide its customers with the best in quality and customer service.	I promise to give you the best in quality and service.

Finally, always write when in a good mood. If you must write when you are irritated or angry, hang on to the draft and revise it when you've calmed down. Regardless of how you try to hide it, your attitude and mood almost always show through in your writing.

Rule 29. Use contractions to warm up your message.

Contractions help make writing conversational and informal, and we encourage you to use them.

Deciding when to use a contraction or when to use the full phrase is a matter of taste and style. Use a contraction whenever you want to achieve a warmer tone in a sentence or when you'd use a contraction if you were speaking the sentence aloud.

This is a problem all of us in financial management face from time to time, is it not?	This is a problem all of us in financial management face from time to time, isn't it?
You can run, but you cannot hide.	You can run, but you can't hide.
Do not make an issue out of it.	Don't make an issue out of it.

When you want a more aloof or remote tone or want to add special emphasis to a phrase, use the written-out phrase.

I won't tolerate prejudice in my department.	I will not tolerate prejudice in my department.

Although contractions make writing conversational, it's possible to overuse them. If you find your writing contains too many contractions, replace a few of them with the written-out phrase.

I don't believe you're the only one who's discovered that Frank's rules can't be broken.	I don't believe you are the only one who has discovered that Frank's rules can't be broken.
It's a known fact that he's the best engineer they've got.	It's a known fact that he is the best engineer they've got.

Rule 30. Avoid unnecessary hedging.

A hedge is a word or phrase that serves as a qualifier, indicating that the author is unsure of the accuracy of the statement that follows and is unwilling to present it as the absolute truth.

Some common hedge words and phrases:

in my opinion
I think
as our records indicate
to the best of my recollection
as I recall
I would guess that
as I understand it
it is my understanding that
it is my considered opinion that
my best guess is that
probably
likely
under the circumstances
if it were mine to do
almost
might
could

well, maybe
may or may not be
is considered to be
regarded as
virtually
practically
probably
I imagine
under these circumstances
hopefully
in some cases
it has been my observation that
for all intents and purposes
try

While hedges are sometimes necessary to separate fact from opinion (see Rule 13), they weaken writing when they're used to avoid responsibility or obscure lack of commitment or inadequate information. Readers mistrust writers who use hedges in every sentence to evade honest and straightforward expression. Sentences are made stronger and more authoritative when the hedge word or phrase is removed.

The error was probably made by the data entry clerk.	The data entry clerk made the error.
I'll try to get the report on your desk by Friday.	I'll have the report on your desk by Friday.
I'll write the ad today if my computer doesn't go down.	I'll write the ad today.
The O-rings quite possibly caused the system leakage.	The O-rings caused the system leakage.
The user should receive the replacement part within a few days or a week at most.	I'll put the replacement part in the mail and send it to the user first-class this afternoon.

Rule 31. Avoid sarcasm.

People write sarcastic letters either to vent their anger or to shame the reader into action. Sarcasm certainly helps vent anger, but it rarely gains cooperation. More often, it creates more anger and gets you fighting with, rather than working with, the other person.

Avoid sarcasm in your writing, especially when writing letters and memos concerning disputes, complaints, or problems. Go through your first draft and delete any sarcastic sentences or phrases. This will make your writing more straightforward, dignified, direct, and persuasive.

Jenny has been an employee at National Bolt Co. for over twenty-five years and a member of your union since its formation. Obviously, this means little to you.

Now I think it is up to the union to make the grand and very generous offer to forget your $189.33 accounting error and waive whatever policy prevents you from paying Jenny her pension, such that it is.

Since my product is strictly for writers, I can't for the life of me understand why you think I should advertise it in *Freelance Graphic Artist Today* magazine.

Jenny has been an employee at National Bolt Co. for over twenty-five years and a member of your union since its formation.

Now I think it is up to the union to forget the $189.33 accounting error and waive whatever policy prevents you from paying Jenny her pension.

Since my product is strictly for writers, I don't understand why you think I should advertise it in *Freelance Graphic Artist Today* magazine.

In your letter of March 3 you state you are an expert in this field, with ten years' experience. Excuse me, then, for even daring to question the work of such a world-class expert. Obviously there is nothing I as a mere employee of your client company with twenty years' experience in our industry could contribute to the development of this project, and so we are returning your materials to you and consider the contract canceled.

I realize you're an expert, but that doesn't mean our point of view isn't valid. My feeling is you have brushed off our comments without really considering them. Am I wrong? I would like to discuss this with you so we can get our relationship back on the right track and get the project going.

5

Principles of Persuasion

The major difference between writing to inform and writing to persuade is one of *intent*. The hallmarks of expository writing are clarity, precision, and organization. Most business writing goes one step beyond the mere transmission of information and seeks to change behavior, attitude, or belief or to motivate the reader to take some specific action.

A sales letter, for example, might be written to get the prospect to agree to an appointment with a sales representative.

A collection letter seeks payment or at least an explanation of why the buyer has not honored the invoice.

A report containing a set of recommendations may, on the surface, appear to be primarily informational, but the author's true motive may be to get management to approve and implement the recommendations made.

A plan or budget is usually thought of as a management tool, but most of them are, in fact, sales documents that seek executive approval of the activities of a department or group within the corporation.

Good proposals don't merely answer questions in the **RFP** (request for proposal); they also make the case why the proposal writer's firm should be awarded the contract.

Some memos simply transmit information, but most contain a request that the writer hopes to persuade the reader to grant.

Even fliers posted on the company bulletin board are written to persuade employees to donate blood, participate in an event, or submit their expense vouchers on time.

This chapter covers some basic principles of persuasive writing designed to elicit from your reader the response you desire.

Rule 32. Gain your reader's attention in an appropriate manner.

To be persuasive, you must get the reader's attention. Readers cannot be swayed by your writing if they don't stop to read it.

But attention must be gained in an appropriate manner. By *appropriate* we mean in a way that logically connects to the main proposition of the letter, memo, or report.

Many inexperienced writers, thinking that the way to gain attention is to be different, use openings that are in no way related to the audience or the message. Doing so conveys a lack of professionalism, makes the writer look foolish, and can be downright offensive.

LIVE NUDE DANCERS! Now that I have your attention . . .	Re: A new way to increase sales of the XR-50 copier

In the example on the left, the writer seeks to gain attention using that favorite tactic of rank amateurs: a sexual reference that has nothing to do with the issue at hand. The result is an absurdity. Outrageous attention-getting devices can work, *but only when they're directly relevant to the subject or audience.* Attention getting just for shock value may attract readers initially. But they will quickly lose interest when they discover that the document in no way relates to the lead or headline.

Here are some appropriate ways to get attention in business documents:

Use a headline. A Re: line in a letter ("Re: Your request for a dental plan") or even a headline typed in all caps and centered on the first page of a memo ("UPDATE ON PROPOSED FAMILY DAY PICNIC") grabs the eye and gets readers reading.

Tell your readers something they already know. Telling your readers something they already know creates empathy. It also gives the impression that you know what you're talking about.

> Dear Racehorse Owner:
>
> No one has to tell you how tough the racing game is. Hazards and heartbreaks abound. Yet today, perhaps as never before, it is possible to profit handsomely from racing even if the horses you own are considered cheap. . . .

By telling readers what they already know, you create a powerful lure that draws them into your copy. Readers like nothing better than to read about themselves and people like them. Tell them what they know, and if it's important, they'll be hooked.

This technique is effective because it reassures readers that they are in familiar company. You establish credibility because you demonstrate that you and the reader share common knowledge, background, interests, or experience.

The most important thing to most people is themselves—their needs, their fears, their hopes, their desires, their ambitions, their concerns. If a letter says, in effect, to the reader, "This is all about *you*," you have guaranteed yourself an attentive audience.

Don't overdo it, though. Don't go on *too* long with the familiar before getting to your point or moving on to new territory. Otherwise, you risk boring your readers and wasting their time. Once they're convinced that you know what you're talking about and understand their situation or their desires, they want to hear what *you* have to say. They want the news, the answer, the solution, the proposition you are offering. They want something new, not something they already know.

Tell them what they don't know. Equally effective is the opposite approach: to tell the reader something he or she doesn't know, something that presents important news or new information that the reader is likely to want to learn more about.

> Dear MIS Director:
>
> Right now, even as you read this sentence, hundreds of valuable computer files are being erased—totally as a result of technical errors built into DASD equipment—in thousands of tape drives throughout the country, possibly including *yours.* Fortunately, now there's a solution that can eliminate accidental tape overwrites forever.

Here the writer alerts the reader to a problem he or she probably has but doesn't know about. People are usually interested in new information if the information relates to their concerns and is important, as is the case in this example.

After telling the readers something they don't know, you should either *prove* what you just said (in case your reader is skeptical) or offer a solution (if the news contains a problem or headache).

Ask a provocative question. Asking questions can be extremely effective in engaging the attention of a busy manager.

> What do Japanese managers have that American managers sometimes lack?

You can ask a question the reader genuinely wants to learn the answer to:

When an employee gets sick, how long does it take your company to recover?

What does it cost to create a brochure? Design a booklet? Develop a newsletter? Produce a press-party invitation? Prepare a sales promotional flip chart?

You can challenge the reader's conventions, attitudes, or beliefs with a provocative question:

Is free-lance a dirty word to you? It really shouldn't be. . . .

It is also effective to ask a question to which the reader must answer yes:

If I could show you a way to reduce your business overhead by 40 percent, would you be interested?

Would you like to own a business, with people waiting in line scrambling to buy from you?

Avoid questions that may invite a no answer:

Are you interested in what XYZ car company has been up to lately?

Also avoid questions on topics of indifference to the reader. Asking such a question is likely to elicit a sarcastic "Who cares?" and get your document tossed into the round file.

Do you know which Oregon architectural firm won this year's Golden Tower Award from the Oregon Society of Architects and Engineers?

Make a startling statement. A statement that shocks or surprises the reader can be an effective attention getter provided the content is related to the main proposition or message of the letter.

R&B Supermarket is going out of business!

By the year 2000, gasoline in our area of the country will cost $5.60 per gallon. . . .

A variation of this technique is to inject a fascinating but little-known statistic.

> Of the 1.5 million PC users in business today, over 95 percent do not know how to touch-type and can operate their keyboards only by using the hunt-and-peck method.
>
> Now, our "Touch-Typing for PC Users" training course can help make every PC user in your organization *much* more productive. . . .

> Our recent fund-raising letter generated a 3.5 percent response from new donors. This may not sound like much, but it's impressive when you realize that the average response to fund-raising letters in recent years has been 1 percent, which is down from the 2 percent that was the average response rate five to six years ago.

> Enclosed are the results from your latest Customer Service Survey. Among the key findings:
>
> • 87 percent of our customers rate our support either "excellent" or "good."
> • The average response time to service calls is twenty-two minutes.
> • When compared with the competition, we rated number one among the five largest system vendors in terms of quality of service and support.

The benefit of including a new fact or statistic in your lead is that people are fascinated with statistics and may keep your letter as reference material instead of throwing it away.

Use an anecdote. Stories gain attention, help readers visualize your message, and add a sense of immediacy.

> Picture this: Your typewriter breaks a day before your proposal is due. . . .

> Three years ago this month, a man I know—he was then a vice-president of a big corporation in Illinois—walked into his boss's

office and handed in his resignation. Two weeks later, he started his own company. . . .

Say something timely. If your busy readers feel they can put aside your letter for later reading, they will. Saying something timely creates a sense of urgency.

Dear Client:

There are five things you can still do to reduce your tax bill this year. But with the end of the year fast approaching, you've got to act on these recommendations within the next two weeks or you'll lose the opportunity altogether.

Consolidated Envelope Manufacturers will be raising prices on all envelopes and packaging materials starting the first of December, which is less than two weeks from today. Therefore, we must make an immediate decision on the quantity and timing of ordering envelopes and packaging materials for the fulfillment center operations. Specifically, should we buy supplies as needed on a just-in-time basis and pay the price increase? Or should we buy now at the lower rates and keep large quantities on hand?

Rule 33. Awaken a need for an idea before presenting the idea.

In persuasive business documents, you must make sure your readers perceive a *need* for your idea, service, product, or organization before presenting the facts and features. If you start talking about widgets without establishing that readers want or even care about widgets, you'll lose them fast.

Even if you know your readers have a need or desire for what you're offering, you must still remind them of this fact. Why? Because they're busy, and they have many things to worry about today. They're not thinking about widgets when they open your letter. So you've got to remind them that they care about widgets and the benefits of widgets before you can sell them widgets.

As plant manager, you know it pays to make every process in your plant run as efficiently as possible. Are yours? With the new quarter-turn Yale widget valve . . .

I haven't heard from you in a while, so I thought I'd drop you a short note. Have you given any further thought to the materials recovery system we discussed? We're still losing about $450 worth of platinum catalyst per day just in Plant B, and with the economy being what it is, I'd love to be able to recover and reuse or resell that material instead of flushing it into the waste stream.

I know you're busy, but I also know there are a lot of improvements you'd like to see made to the current company phone system—more lines, more features, fewer lost calls. But we in Telecommunications can't make those improvements unless you tell us what you need. That's why it's important that you fill out the brief Telecom Audit Form we sent you last month. A duplicate is attached. . . .

And what about readers who do *not* realize they have a need or desire for what you're offering? It's your job to convince them that the need exists before you can sell them on your offer.

Dear Personnel Director:

Employee theft may not seem like a big problem to you right now. After all, what do a few missing pads, pencils, or paper clips mean to a large corporation like XYZ?

Think again. According to industry estimates, firms of your size are losing $10,000 *daily* from stealing. And that's just *small* items like office supplies and free photocopies. Fortunately, now there's a new system for monitoring and controlling those expensive "freebies" and "perks" that are costing you so much. . . .

The key to persuasive writing is to intensify the reader's response first to his or her basic need or problem, then to the exclusive solution you offer to satisfy the need or solve the problem.

After bringing the need to the reader's attention, you should leave the reader thinking, *I know I have a need, but what can I do about it?* Then offer your idea or product as the solution.

If you don't have a service contract on your typewriter, you have two choices: (1) panic or (2) pay hefty repair bills. Now, with our service contract, you pay only one low fee for a full-year guarantee that your typewriter will work when you need it.

If you and the other department managers will take a few minutes to complete and return the Telecom Audit Form we sent, we will be able to make significant improvements and upgrades in the company telephone system by the first quarter of next year.

We find we have an extra $25,000 in the Plant B equipment budget. With some additional funds from your group, we would be able to install and have the recovery system running in three months. Payback for the cost of installation would take less than four months.

Rule 34. Stress benefits, not features.

A purely factual description of a product, service, or idea lists its features. What the user of the product or service gains as a result of the features is *benefits*.

A feature of your new microcomputer, for example, might be that it contains the XL-9000 microprocessor chip. The benefit is that the chip allows it to run software five times faster than conventional models so that the user can get more work done in less time.

As a rule, people seek benefits, not features. By emphasizing benefits, you address the heart of persuasion: self-interest. The reader's primary concern is "What's in it for me?"

Consider the purchase of workstations as an example. The company manager wants the workstation that will boost productivity. The secretary, if given a choice, prefers the workstation that is easiest to use and reduces eyestrain and elbow strain. The people you write to are primarily interested in how your proposition personally benefits them.

When writing to persuade, stress the benefits the readers will get from your proposition, not the proposition itself.

All employees are invited to attend Family Day this Saturday and are encouraged to bring friends and family.	All employees are invited to attend Family Day this Saturday and are encouraged to bring friends and family. There will be food, games, and prizes for all! Plus a tour of the plant.
I'd like to drop by your office to have a short chat with you.	I'd like to drop by your office to have a short chat with you about what we can do to avoid a repeat of last month's accounting disaster.
Our computer system tracks your forms usage on a daily, weekly, or monthly basis and generates management reports that are delivered via hard copy or facsimile on a timely basis.	We keep track of your forms usage and tell you when it's time to reorder. This way, you don't have to worry about checking inventory levels, and you will never run out.
The Fax-800 has full broadcast and polling capabilities with automatic redial.	With the Fax-800, you can run your document through the feeder once and have it faxed to up to 120 different people automatically. If their fax number is busy, the Fax-800 will automatically redial until it gets through.

Rule 35. Use facts, opinions, and statistics to prove your case.

Do not expect readers to readily accept every statement you make as the truth. Many people are skeptical; most want proof.

At worst, some of your readers will be openly hostile to your proposition. Factory workers who fear that robots will put them out of work will not take kindly to an announcement of your new factory automation program. Executives who think typing on a keyboard is something a secretary should do will resist the efforts of the training department to teach them how to use desktop microcomputers. You must give people—especially those likely to be hostile to your ideas—a reason to believe you before they'll listen seriously.

Use facts to support your claims or recommendations:

> My recommendation is to stop running two-page ads and replace all current two-page spreads with more cost effective one-page ads. I know Jerry thinks two-page spreads are more noticeable. But according to a survey published in the advertising column of the *New York Times*, two-page ads get only 30 percent more readership than single pages, yet cost twice as much. The research concludes, "Single-page ads are by far the better buy."

When you have the information available, cite the source or authority supporting your factual claim, especially if you believe it will be called into question.

> The home-office market will expand dramatically in the coming decade. The Roper Organization projects that within five years there will be 20 million full-time home-based businesses in the United States. And a survey conducted by Link Resources Group found that of the 89 million households in the United States, 16 million already have one or more home workers.

If facts and statistics are not readily available, give an opinion to support your claim. The more the readers perceive that you are an expert in the field, the more readily they will accept your opinion as the truth.

> In ten years working in the telecommunications field, with more than twenty-five major T-1 network implementations, I've learned that the vendor's field service and support are at least as important as the technical features of their equipment.

If you don't have credentials, at least give a logical reason why you believe your claim is valid.

> I've called twelve firms that exhibited in last year's Peat Moss Makers Exhibition, and they all felt it was a total waste of time and money.

Giving an opinion unsupported by facts, statistics, logic, common sense, the reader's experience, or everyday observation is the least persuasive way of writing. When you simply say, "I don't think we should exhibit at the Peat Moss Makers Exhibition," your boss will immediately challenge, "Why not?"

Frequently, the ability to write a persuasive letter or memo hinges not on style but on research: the gathering of facts, arguments, and statistics to support your position. One of the biggest shortcomings of business writers is laziness or lack of time. They are not *unable* to research and write persuasively; they are simply unwilling to do so, or they haven't the time. But if you want to persuade your readers, you must support your arguments with facts.

Rule 36. Don't get bogged down in unnecessary details or arguments.

Facts and logical arguments can help make your case, but don't overdo it. *Selective* use of facts and statistics can strengthen your writing, turning a weak plea for compliance into a powerful, persuasive request that gets readers to react. But overload the readers with facts—tell them *too much*—and you'll lose them.

Business writers, especially those dealing in technical areas, have a tendency to want to tell readers everything when instead they should be telling them only what they, the readers, want and need to know. Use facts with restraint. Make sure the information is complete, but do not belabor your point. Remove all unnecessary detail.

The program, written in approximately 150,000 lines of C code, was developed at Oxford over a period of eighteen months by a team of programmers, scientists, and mathematicians who worked together to design the software to allow the user to do complex mathematical calculations on a personal computer.	The program is designed to allow you to do complex mathematical calculations right on your PC.
Our product line includes the following types of level detectors: beam breaker, capacitance, conductive, differential pressure, hydrostatic pressure, infrared, microwave, R-F admittance, sonic echo, thermal, and weight and cable level detectors that are described in the enclosed catalog.	We offer a full line of level detectors, as described in the enclosed catalog.

Statistics, too, should be used with restraint. A few key numbers help make the point; if you have a lot of numbers to present, place them in tables or appendixes.

Rule 37. Tell the reader what to do next.

Now that you have your reader contemplating all the benefits of your idea, proposal, product, or service, you are ready to suggest further action. The reader may not know what to do next even if interested in what you're offering. So provide guidance.

This can be done lightly ("Let's discuss this further at your convenience"; "I look forward to hearing from you") or more assertively ("If you purchase your support contract this week, we'll take 10 percent off the regular price"; "Can we begin the work this month?"; "When would be a good time for us to drop by and discuss your plans in more detail?"; "We will send a contract for your signature today by overnight courier").

Give the reader a reason to act now instead of later, if possible. People will avoid taking action if they can find the slightest excuse to do so. Some ways to generate immediate action:

- Tell the reader why a minor delay now may result in a major delay later. ("He is going on vacation for two weeks in December, so if we don't get the preliminary drawings to him this week, he won't be able to start until after Christmas.")
- Offer an incentive for immediate action. ("Retain me for this consultation within the next ten days and I'll throw in any three reports from my *Writer's Profit Catalog* at no extra charge.")
- Tell them the negative consequences that will result if they *don't* take action. ("If we don't settle this complaint quickly, we'll get a lot of negative publicity.")
- Set a time limit or other limitation on your offer. ("I'm offering this service only to the first six of my existing clients who call me in response to this letter.")
- If you desire cooperation of the reader's immediate supervisor or someone else higher up in the corporate hierarchy, gently remind the reader of it. ("Don Eckley said it was really important to get your input on this project.")

Rule 38. Before making a request, give the reader a reason to respond.

When making requests, appeal to the reader's self-interest. Give the reader a reason why it will pay to do as you ask. Be specific. And use facts to support your arguments.

We hope you will support the Ad Club by attending the October meeting and the special presentation from speaker Bob Rorke.	Be sure to attend the October meeting so you won't miss nationally known creative consultant Bob Rorke's presentation, "Ten Ways to Immediately Generate More Sales and Profits from All Your Advertising."
The Red Cross needs your help.	Someday you may need the Red Cross. But right now the Red Cross needs *you*.
I'd like to meet with you to present our company's product line to you and make you familiar with what we offer.	I'd like to meet with you to show you how our company's full line of emission-control equipment can help control pollution and reduce energy costs in your plant.

Even instructional writing must contain some degree of motivation. Insurance companies, for example, know that saying, "Please complete and mail this form today," is not persuasive enough, because many policyholders give low priority to filling out medical claim forms.

Please complete and mail the enclosed form today.	To speed processing of your claim, please complete and mail this form today.

Be sure to call the phone company and give them your ringer equivalent number once the Answer-Back 100 phone machine is installed on your line.	Be sure to call the phone company and give them your ringer equivalent number once the Answer-Back 100 phone machine is installed on your line. Otherwise, you may lose some calls or messages.
Insert knob A in hole B. Do not force. Lubricate if necessary.	Insert knob A in hole B. Do not force or the attachment will break. Lubricate if necessary.

Rule 39. Do not assume the reader has been persuaded by your argument.

Do not assume the reader has been persuaded by what you've written. If you indicate that you think your reader has been convinced (or should have been convinced) when that's not the case, you're likely to elicit your reader's pointed *disagreement* with you.

Three phrases in particular are presumptuous if used carelessly. They should be used with caution or not at all:

As you know . . .
I'm sure you'll agree . . .
I need you to . . .

The first of these phrases is dangerous when used to introduce an opinion masquerading as fact; for example, "As you know, the excellence of the training department is what drives the success of Alpert International." The reader, a district sales manager, will undoubtedly think, No, I *don't* know that; I think it's *sales*, not training, that makes the company successful, and will read with an attitude of challenge and hostility.

Using "As you know" when introducing a fact is also dangerous because you're assuming the reader knows the fact and accepts it as the truth—which may not be the case. To avoid this, replace "As you know" with "As you *may* know."

As you know, 80 percent of all managers accept the 7-S theory.	As you may know, 80 percent of all managers accept the 7-S theory.

Use "As you know" only when

- you know that your reader knows what will follow.
- it is flattering to the reader to be presumed to know what will follow.
- your reader is of like mind and shares your opinion or view.

Another dangerous phrase is "I'm sure you'll agree." This is often used as a fallback position by writers who, knowing they haven't made a persuasive argument, think they can bully their readers into accepting their proposition simply by telling them they've been persuaded. "I'm sure you'll agree" really says, *You have to agree with me because I want you to—even though I know I haven't really proved what I'm saying.*

"I'm sure you agree" *can* be used effectively when you are trying to make your readers aware that their position is unreasonable or unproductive and you want to get them on your side. For example: "I'm sure you'll agree we're both negotiating in good faith and want what is best for the company," or "I'm sure you'll agree that we don't want to promote discrimination here." You can get approval and then proceed. The main point: Don't write "I'm sure you'll agree" unless you're actually sure your reader *will* agree. Don't presume without a basis for doing so.

Another variation of "I'm sure you'll agree" is "I'm sure you've heard of," as in "I'm sure you've heard of [our company, product, or service]." If you're not selling a major brand or you don't work for one of the Fortune 500, the chances are the reader's response will be a smug "No, I *haven't* heard of you. Who do you think you are, anyway?" Replace "I'm sure you've heard of" with "Have you heard of?"

I'm with James Jones Financial Investment Group. I'm sure you've heard of us . . .	I'm with James Jones Financial Investment Group. Have you heard of us?

Perhaps the worst offender of the lot is "I need you to. . ." Implicit in this phrase is the assumption (erroneous) that *your* needs supersede those of the reader. In fact, the opposite is true: People are most easily persuaded when you satisfy what *they* want and what *they* need, not what you want or need. "I need you to" says to your reader," *I know I haven't persuaded you, so I'm just going to command you.* It seldom works.

"I need you to" should be replaced by "Would you please," "Please," or a logical reason why the reader should comply with your request.

I need you to stay late tonight and type up these briefs.	Would you please stay late tonight and type up these briefs?
I need you to send all branch managers a copy of the first draft of the user's manual.	Please send all branch managers a copy of the first draft of the user's manual.
I need you to sign this contract and mail it back to me.	Your signature will give me the go-ahead to begin work on your project.

6

Principles of Punctuation, Grammar, Abbreviation, Capitalization, and Spelling

Why is it that so many business documents contain errors in punctuation, grammar, abbreviation, capitalization, and spelling?

Some errors are predictable; they occur because the rules themselves provide only tenuous guidelines. Other errors stem from the confusion we experienced when drilled in what seemed like countless arcane rules involving clauses, prepositions, and pronouns.

Businesspeople may not need to know the nuances of every principle of grammar to do their jobs well, but they do need the basics. This chapter gives the essential rules guiding the use of the main punctuation marks, grammar principles, and abbreviation and capitalization rules.

When it comes to spelling, most businesspeople would be wasting their time trying to learn the exception-ridden rules of spelling. Better to just memorize the 50–100 words that almost everyone misspells (and also buy a spelling checker for your word processor).

Punctuation

Rule 40. Use commas to indicate a brief pause.

Commas are used so frequently and in such a wide variety of situations that readers wishing a *comprehensive* guide to their use should consult books on punctuation and grammar. Among the best sources are *The Careful Writer* by Theodore Bernstein (Atheneum, 1965); *The Chicago Manual of Style* (University of Chicago Press, 1982); *English Grammar and Composition* by John E. Warriner and Francis Griffith (Harcourt Brace & World, 1965); and *Words into Type* (Prentice-Hall, 1974).

Our purpose is to pare down this large topic, choosing selected comma principles, definitions, and examples that lend themselves to the world of memos, letters, and reports.

It isn't easy to generalize about the functions of commas except to say that they indicate a brief pause or that they group words that belong together. At various times, the comma joins, encloses, or separates the parts of a sentence. The following principles guide your use of the comma in common situations faced by business writers.

Use commas to separate items in a series.

The items in a series may be words, phrases, or clauses. The last item is usually preceded by a conjunction, such as *and, but,* or *or.* When no conjunction is used to connect the last item in a series, the last item is still separated by a comma.

> I'm interested in investing in stocks, bonds, or mutual funds.

> Hounded by the press, unable to focus on his job, pressured by the board, Tomkins resigned last Thursday.

> I sent out press releases, John wrote ads, and the rest of us put together direct mail packages.

Use a comma before the final item in a series.

Some writers omit the final comma before the conjunction in a series. They believe that the final comma is not needed because the conjunction provides an adequate pause. There is still some debate about whether the final comma before the "and," "or," or "but" in a series is necessary. Newspapers tend to omit it; books tend to use it. We believe, as do Strunk and White, that the final comma provides insurance against misreading.

The mail carriers agreed they would need bicycles, motorized bikes and scooters.	The mail carriers agreed they would need bicycles, motorized bikes, and scooters.

In the sentence on the left above, there is some doubt as to whether the scooters as well as the bikes are motorized.

The entertainment committee booked Barry Manilow, Gladys Knight and the Pips and Neil Diamond for our annual convention.	The entertainment committee booked Barry Manilow, Gladys Knight and the Pips, and Neil Diamond for our annual convention.

The comma in the right-hand example above prevents readers from expecting to hear the group "the Pips and Neil Diamond" at their annual convention. In a sentence that begins with a series of names, the final comma is again necessary to avoid a misreading:

Bill, Barry and Susan will prepare the presentation.	Bill, Barry, and Susan will prepare the presentation.

In the left-hand example above, it's not clear whether the writer is informing Bill that Barry and Susan will prepare the presentation or informing the reader that the three people named will prepare the presentation.

Use a comma to separate two or more adjectives that each modifies a noun.

It was a short, informal meeting.

We sat through a dull, repetitive meeting.

Do not place a comma between the two adjectives if the final adjective acts as a unit with the noun.

It was a crisp autumn day.

We attended the paralegal orientation meeting.

In the first example, the adjective *autumn* acts as a unit with the noun *day*, so there is no comma between *crisp* and *autumn*.

One way to remember this is to test whether you could logically link the two adjectives with "and." If so ("It was a short and informal meeting"), use the comma. If inserting the "and" makes the sentence absurd ("It was a crisp and autumn day"), don't use the comma.

Use a comma to separate independent clauses joined by a coordinating conjunction.

A clause is a group of words containing a subject and predicate used as part of a sentence. Those that express a complete thought and can stand alone if removed from their sentences are called *independent* clauses; those that do not express a complete thought and cannot stand alone are called *dependent* or *subordinate* clauses.

In the sentence "Although John invested in stocks, Mary invested in bonds," *Mary invested in bonds* is an independent clause because it can stand alone as a sentence. *Although John invested in stocks* is a dependent clause because it cannot stand alone as a sentence.

Use commas to separate independent clauses joined by a coordinating conjunction *(and, or, but, nor, for,* or *yet)* unless the clauses are very short.

The *Tribune* has seven reporters, and they are hiring two new reporters on Monday.

The outline was good, but the final proposal was too long.

The telephone system works well, yet it probably will cost twice as much as the earlier system.

Peter spoke and Ellen showed slides.

Use a comma to separate a long introductory clause from the rest of the sentence.

Use a comma to separate from the rest of the sentence a long introductory clause, subordinate clause, or introductory words such as "well," "yes," "however," "therefore," and "moreover."

After reviewing your résumé and talking with several of your references, we are happy to offer you the position of sales manager.

Reading and revising the manuscript, I discovered a new way to outline Chapter 4.

Yes, I'd be happy to invest in a no-load fund that paid 10 percent interest.

Use commas to set off parenthetic or nonrestrictive modifiers in a sentence.

A nonrestrictive phrase or clause is one that is not essential to the meaning of the sentence but merely adds an idea to the sentence. Nonrestrictive elements are set off by commas.

The company library, where you can find past annual reports, has been moved to the twenty-first floor.

A restrictive phrase, on the other hand, is essential to the sentence; to omit it would alter the meaning of the sentence. Restrictive phrases and clauses are not set off by commas.

Tom Martin is the only Acme director *who voted for the resolution.*

We look forward to the day *when we can sign the contracts.*

Give it to the secretary *whose desk is across the hall.*

Notice how a comma would alter the meaning in the last example above.

Give it to the secretary, whose desk is across the hall.

With a comma, the sentence gives information about the

location of the secretary's desk—across the hall. Without the comma, the sentence tells you which of several secretaries should be given the memo—the one whose desk is across the hall rather than one whose desk is elsewhere.

Use a comma to indicate omission of words that are understood.

Laura is in charge of professional staff; Jay, support staff.

In this sentence, it is understood that Jay *is in charge of* support staff.

Use commas to set off geographic terms and to separate the date from the year.

Kansas City, Missouri

July 25, 1992

The plant in Trenton, New Jersey, will reopen next year.

Exception: Omit the comma between the month and the year.

July 1992

Rule 41. Use a semicolon to separate independent clauses not joined by a conjunction.

Semicolons do just the opposite of what commas do: They separate *independent* clauses. An independent clause, containing a subject and a verb, can stand on its own. What, then, does a semicolon do that a period does not do?

First, a semicolon is used to separate independent thoughts that relate closely to each other and are not linked by a conjunction.

Hundreds of tests are conducted to determine product safety; none prevents accidents altogether.

A semicolon is used instead of a period when two sentences are very closely related.

I will indeed be in Chicago on May 8; however, I will be unable to attend the meeting.

Semicolons can be used to separate phrases or items in a list in which the phrases and items themselves contain commas:

We went to three cities last week: Saint Paul, Minnesota; Salinas, California; and Pueblo, Colorado.

Without the semicolon, confusion results:

Saint Paul, Minnesota, Salinas, California, and Pueblo, Colorado.

Here's another example of how semicolons help group elements in a sentence that belong together:

We hired three new managers: Jacqueline Heyward, manager of management development; Joan Fahrenkrug, director of training; and Barbara Gross, vice-president of human resources.

Rule 42. Use a colon to introduce a list or explanation.

In *West Side Story,* the song "Something's Coming" sets the scene for much of the action that follows. In punctuation, colons signal us that "something's coming": a list, a long quotation, an explanation, or a business letter.

Use a colon to introduce a list of items.

You will probably have to answer the following questions: How long have you been employed? Why did you leave your last position? What experience do you have?

Go to the stationery store and get me four items: typing paper, typewriter ribbons, correction fluid, and pencils.

Use a colon before a long or formal quotation.

The consultant wrote: "In these times, it is impossible to estimate the impact of poor business writing on national productivity and profitability."

He started his speech by saying: "Unaccustomed as I am to formal speaking . . ."

Use a colon to separate independent clauses when the second clause explains or amplifies the first.

Businesspeople succeed by following an important principle: If you work hard, you'll get ahead.

Hospitals exist for one purpose: to heal the sick.

Use a colon after the salutation of a business letter.

Dear Mr. Stephens:

Dear Credit Manager:

Dear Subscriber:

Exception: When addressing someone by first name, it is acceptable to use a comma after the name.

Dear Larry,

Dear Joan,

Rule 43. Add an apostrophe and an *s* to form the possessive case of a singular noun.

Generally, adding an apostrophe and an *s* is the correct way to form a possessive of a singular noun or a name.

boss's desk
chairman's office
Jones's company
Mr. Karrass's software
Mary's assistant

To form the possessive of a plural noun, add just an apostrophe.

employees' benefits
members' dues

Rule 44. Hyphenate two words compounded to form an adjective modifier if they precede a noun.

When two or more words are compounded to form an adjective, they are hyphenated.

long range goals and objectives	long-range goals and objectives
middle income housing	middle-income housing
state of the art equipment	state-of-the-art equipment
year to date sales	year-to-date sales
year end totals	year-end totals

Hyphens are used in compound modifiers because they help the reader avoid confusion. For example, if a compound such as *first rate seminar* were not hyphenated, the reader might expect *first* to modify the phrase *rate seminar*—meaning that there were a number of "rate seminars" (seminars concerning postal, utility, or some other rates) held and this was the first. When the hyphen is included, it becomes clear the seminar was first-rate in quality.

The hyphen is usually omitted with an adverb ending in *ly*.

artificially inflated interest rates
financially stable organization
technologically advanced civilization

Adjectives ending in *ly* are hyphenated only when used with present participles (words ending in *ing*), as in *friendly-sounding voice*.

Compound words used as adjectives are hyphenated before a noun, but they are *not* hyphenated when they occur after the noun.

| This is my up-to-date report. | Bring them up to date. |
| Here is a list of the out-of-stock items. | C-arms and conductive cushions are listed as out of stock. |

A modifier that would be hyphenated before a noun retains the hyphenation when it follows a noun and a form of the verb *to be (are, is, am, was, were, be, been)*.

He is the results-oriented manager.	Jim is results-oriented.
They served a second-rate meal.	The food was second-rate.
We are required to use EPA-approved and DOE-certified process equipment	Our process is EPA-approved and DOE-certified.

Do not hyphenate scientific terms, chemicals, diseases, and plant and animal names used as unit modifiers if no hyphen appears in their original form. Because *swine flu* does not contain a hyphen, we write "swine flu epidemic," not "swine-flu epidemic." Other examples:

sulfur dioxide emissions
the pulp and paper industry
an apple tree grove.

Two adjacent words are hyphenated if they express a single idea and if, without the hyphen, this idea is not immediately clear. The hyphen is used to join the words into a single noun and make the connection between the two words clearer to the reader.

For example, the unhyphenated combination *feed pipe* seems, at first, to be an imperative to feed a hungry pipe. With the hyphen, we instantly recognize the compound *feed-pipe* as the pipe through which fluids are fed into a process system.

In modern business English, the trend has been first to

join two nouns with a hyphen and then, after they become accepted, to make them a single closed word.

fire place	fire-place	fireplace
stock broker	stock-broker	stockbroker
turn key	turn-key	turnkey
type setting	type-setting	typesetting

The dictionary is the final authority on whether two words are separated, hyphenated, or joined into one word.

Rule 45. Use an ellipsis to show hesitation or omission.

An ellipsis—formed by typing three periods in a row—is used to show hesitation, uncertainty, or reluctance.

I want to buy a personal computer . . . but I'm afraid it will be too difficult to learn.

You can use an ellipsis to indicate an unresolved thought or opinion at the end of a sentence. When you use an ellipsis at the end of a sentence, you type four periods: the period closing the sentence followed by the three periods of the ellipsis.

Johnson says the market for fiberoptics will undergo explosive growth in the coming decade. But I'm not so sure. . . .

An ellipsis is also used to indicate the omission of words from a sentence. This is especially helpful when quoting material from which you only want to use a portion of the text. Use the ellipsis to indicate deletions of words from the original material:

"I hate cat owners but love cats more than anything on the face of the earth," says Dr. James Smith, founder of the New Milford Cat Clinic.

"I . . . love cats more than anything on the face of the earth," says Dr. James Smith, founder of the New Milford Cat Clinic.

Rule 46. Use parentheses to add explanatory material that's not part of the main thought.

Use parentheses to add explanatory material or an aside that is not part of the main thought of a sentence. This can range from a few words to a sentence or two in length. (If it's longer, you may want to put it in a footnote or appendix.)

> The tax law (revised last year) says that consumer interest is no longer fully deductible.

> We sold Jefferson School two used binders. (They did not have the budget to afford a brand-new binder.)

> Because the factory missed the production deadline (it was not their fault; a trucker's strike prevented the raw materials from being delivered in time), the clients canceled their contract with us and are now buying from our competitor.

Periods and commas usually appear outside the parentheses whether the parentheses appear in the middle or at the end of the sentence.

> If you like our daily planning system (samples enclosed), we can customize them with your company name and logo.

> Here are the advertising specialties you ordered (imprinted with your company logo, as requested).

The only time a period is used within parentheses is when the parentheses contain a complete sentence.

> Please send in your order right away. (Our inventory is almost depleted, and the few remaining units will go quickly.)

A question mark or exclamation point can appear inside the parentheses only if it pertains to the parenthetic expression.

> We received your order and will print the wall calendars as soon as we know your color preference. (Do you prefer green, blue, or black?)

Your hot sauce (the best I've ever tasted!) has great market potential, and I'd be interested in featuring it in our next food catalog.

Rule 47. Use a dash to interrupt—or highlight—a thought.

Like an ellipsis, a comma, or parentheses, the dash is used to separate and set off one part of a sentence from the other parts. However, the dash is a more abrupt, more *dramatic* separation.

My golf partner (your boss and the owner of the restaurant in which you are employed) will certainly learn of the shoddy service we received from you Saturday night.	My golf partner—your boss and the owner of the restaurant in which you are employed—will certainly learn of the shoddy service we received from you Saturday night.

The dash is an effective device for highlighting or emphasizing a thought.

A winner never quits, and a quitter never wins.	A winner never quits—and a quitter never wins.
We won the battle and the war.	We won the battle—and the war.

A dash can be used to interrupt a thought and interject another idea into the sentence.

The employee benefits plan needs a major overhaul.	The employee benefits plan —and Tom agrees with me on this point—needs a major overhaul.

In this example, you could also use parentheses. The choice is based on intent: Parentheses keep their contents in the background; dashes place additional emphasis on the idea they contain and make it stand out from the rest of the sentence.

The employee benefits plan (and Tom agrees with me on this point) needs a major overhaul.	The employee benefits plan—and Tom agrees with me on this point—needs a major overhaul.
The success of this project (and you can quote me on this) was due primarily to the use of the new project management software.	The success of this project—and you can quote me on this—was due primarily to the use of the new project management software.

A dash can also be used in place of a colon to introduce explanatory material.

He was right on two counts: Our old ad was terrible, and the new one he wrote is selling like gangbusters.	He was right on two counts—our old ad was terrible, and the new one he wrote is selling like gangbusters.

Modern business writing style allows occasional use of the dash for purely dramatic effect.

We have to prepare a major presentation to a major Fortune 500 prospect by tomorrow.	We have to prepare a major presentation to a major Fortune 500 prospect—by tomorrow.

A warning: Overuse of the dash (or underlining, italics, and other techniques used to make writing more lively) will serve only to reduce its dramatic effect, as in this example:

If you want me to handle the assignment—great. It's an ideal way—for both our companies—to establish a long—and profitable—relationship. Send me the background—quickly. We'll get back to you—with some on-target recommendations— soon. Here's to a successful venture—for both of us!

Rule 48. Avoid slash constructions.

Do not use slash constructions; they sound awkward and unfriendly. Avoid *and/or, either/or, he/she* (which sounds like a brand-name chocolate bar, not a pronoun), and especially *s/he.*

Tom and/or Bill will fly to Florida to make the presentation.	Tom or Bill (or both) will fly to Florida to make the presentation.
If an operator cannot answer a customer's question, he/she should transfer the call to the user support group.	If an operator cannot answer a customer's question, he or she should transfer the call to the user support group.

Rule 49. Put commas inside quotation marks.

When writing dialogue or putting any other words or phrases in quotation marks, place the comma inside the quotation mark (if no other closing punctuation mark is used).

"The H-6000 is the finest device of its kind on the market today," said Bob Jackson, president of the firm.

Modern stockbrokers use "Quotrons," a computerized version of the old ticker-tape machines.

Grammar

Rule 50. Avoid subject and verb disagreement.

We know that singular subjects take singular verbs and that plural subjects take plural verbs. So what could give us any trouble?

For one thing, a phrase that comes between a subject and a verb can throw us off. If the subject is singular but the phrase contains a plural word, the subject and verb should still be singular.

In reference to your recent letter, your address in our files are correct.	In reference to your recent letter, your address in our files is correct.

The subject of the sentence is "address"; the phrase "in our files" is an intervening phrase that should not affect the form of the verb. So, since "address" is singular, the verb should be "is," not "are."

The longer and more complex the subject, the more care you must take to make sure that all parts are in agreement.

Neither of the invited speakers are able to attend.	Neither of the invited speakers is able to attend.
Some residents complained, but the zoning board and most of the community was willing to support the plan.	Some residents complained, but the zoning board and most of the community were willing to support the plan.

In the first example above, "neither" is the subject of the sentence, not "speakers," so the verb must also be singular. In the second sentence, the verb must be plural because the subject ("zoning board and most of the community") is plural.

Rule 51. Avoid improper use of reflexive pronouns.

Personal pronouns combined with *-self* or *-selves* are called *reflexive*. They may be used in two ways. First, they may be used *reflexively*.

John drove himself to the office.

Second, they may be used for emphasis.

John himself prepared the presentation.

Businesspeople tend to use the reflexive form in situations in which it is not necessary.

Margery and myself have been a great help to her.	Margery and I have been a great help to her.

"Myself" is the wrong choice: You wouldn't write "Myself have been a great help to her." Probably the most common error with the reflexive takes place in casual speech. We see someone at the office and ask, "How are you?" The person replies, "Fine. And yourself?" That's wrong. The reply should be "Fine. And you?"

We're not sure how this error originated, but it may have something to do with a subtle perception that words like "you" or "me" are too informal. They are usually the right words; reflexives are correct in very few situations. Here are a few examples of the correct use of the reflexive:

We did it ourselves.

John voted for himself.

Speaking for myself, I would change the organizational structure.

Rule 52. Avoid sentence fragments and run-on sentences.

A group of words is a complete sentence when it has a subject and a verb and expresses a complete thought. Conversely, a sentence fragment is a group of words that does not express a complete thought. It should not be allowed to stand by itself, but should be kept in the sentence of which it is a part:

As we discussed in our telephone conversation of December 21, 1990, in which I requested a photocopy of a check drawn on the public assistance account.	As we discussed in our telephone conversation of December 21, 1990, in which I requested a photocopy of a check drawn on the public assistance account, I need to research how the check was applied.

In the incorrect example, the writer got so carried away with all the details that he or she forgot to include a subject and a verb. The subject is "I" and the verb is "need."

When a comma is used between two complete sentences, the result is referred to as a "run-on" sentence. One sentence is permitted to "run on" into the next:

The *Tribune* has six stackers, they have ordered two more.	The *Tribune* has six stackers, and they have ordered two more.
	The *Tribune* has six stackers and has ordered two more.

You could also solve the problem by putting a semicolon between the two clauses:

The *Tribune* has six stackers; they have ordered two more.

Run-on sentences using "however" are especially common:

Orders are increasing rapidly, however, our inventory is low.	Orders are increasing rapidly; however, our inventory is low.
I went to see our sales manager, however, he was out of town.	I went to see our sales manager; however, he was out of town.

The "however" in each of these sentences is the first word of the second independent clause. It is not a parenthetic "however" as in the sentence "Tom, however, will not be promoted."

Is there a correct use for a sentence fragment? Yes. Sentence fragments can be dramatic, attention-getting tags to thoughts. Maybe that's why the advertising world is so fond of them. For example, one newspaper's slogan is "We cover your world. All of it." Of course, "all of it" is, technically, a sentence fragment. But it still provides added force to the slogan—greater force, perhaps, than a complete sentence would.

Our advice is to reserve the use of sentence fragments for appropriate situations (e.g., sales letters or advertisements) and even then to use them sparingly, if at all.

Rule 53. Avoid dangling modifiers.

To modify is to limit. A modifying phrase or clause must sensibly define or limit the meaning of a word or phrase in

a sentence. If we wrote, "As constructed, the agreement doesn't protect you," the modifying phrase "As constructed" clearly modifies *the agreement.*
When the phrase or clause doesn't modify the subject of the sentence, then the modifier is "dangling." In the following example, "As a new citizen" at first modifies "I":

> As a new citizen, I'd like to welcome you to our shores.

This is correct only if *you* are the new citizen. If the new citizen is the person you're welcoming, though, say:

> I'd like to welcome you as a new citizen to our shores.

Many dangling modifiers can be corrected simply by making the second half of the sentence active.

Having found the missing report, the search was ended by the secretary.	Having found the missing report, the secretary ended the search.

In this sentence, the phrase "the search" could not have found the missing report. If you change the sentence to the active voice, the word "secretary" becomes the subject of the sentence and is capable of finding the missing report. Here's another example:

> After agreeing to stay late, the cluttered file drawer was cleaned out by the new employee.

This sentence makes it seem as if the cluttered file drawer agreed to stay late. By making the sentence active, the writer eliminates the dangling modifier.

> After agreeing to stay late, the new employee cleaned out the cluttered file drawer.

Some dangling modifiers can be corrected by rephrasing the introductory clause:

When choosing a designer, talent should be your priority.	When you choose a designer, talent should be your priority.
When choosing a designer, your priority should be talent.	When you choose a designer, your priority should be talent.

Who is choosing the designer? The left-hand examples above suggest that "talent" or "your priority" is doing the choosing.

Often, rephrasing the subject of the sentence is necessary:

When choosing a designer, talent should be your priority.	When choosing a designer, make talent your priority.
As manager of the branch that holds your checking account, your November ninth letter to Mr. Kaback was sent to me.	As manager of the branch that holds your checking account, I've been given your November ninth letter to Mr. Kaback.

Obviously, the "November ninth letter" is not the "manager of the branch that holds your checking account."

Rule 54. Avoid misplaced modifiers.

An awkward arrangement of modifiers can make a sentence confusing (e.g., "The checks are on the desk, which you need to cash quickly"). Although a modifier should clarify or limit the word it modifies, the effect of the modifier may be lost or diverted to some other word. This happens because the modifier is placed too far from the word it is supposed to modify or because it is placed where it might modify either of two different words or phrases.

Always place modifiers as close as possible to the words they modify. A misplaced modifier may force the reader to reread the sentence to be sure what it says:

| I want a typewriter for my secretary, preferably with memory. | I want a typewriter, preferably with memory, for my secretary. |

The modifier "preferably with memory" needs to be placed next to the word it modifies: "typewriter." Misplaced modifiers leave your reader guessing what you mean to say.

| I have enclosed two checks that represent interest on the matured certificates that you have not previously received. | I have enclosed two checks that represent interest you have not previously received on matured certificates. |

What does "that you have not previously received" refer to—the interest or the certificates? The sentence at right above makes it clear.

Another example

| We added your figures for premiums due on the spread sheet and compared that total to several other totals. | On the spread sheet, we added your figures for premiums due and compared that total to several other totals. |

The sentence on the left makes it seem as though the premiums are due on the spread sheet. When "On the spread sheet" starts the sentence, the confusion is eliminated.

Abbreviations

Rule 55. Use too few abbreviations rather than too many.

Most business writers are overly fond of abbreviations and acronyms—much to the detriment of their writing. Abbreviations may save time by eliminating the need to write a lengthy title or phrase over and over again. Unfortunately, trying to read a document filled with abbreviations is like trying to decipher a secret message without knowing the code: It's almost impossible.

When we rely on abbreviations in our business writing, we start a process of "inbreeding" that may prevent us from clearly communicating our thoughts to people outside our company, department, or discipline. Readers are intimidated when they see a bunch of abbreviations; rather than risk embarrassment by asking you what the abbreviations stand for, they'll read without really comprehending your message (or will skip your document altogether).

To make your writing clear, use abbreviations sparingly and explain every abbreviation you do use. Always define an abbreviation the first time you use it.

If the written-out word is more familiar than the initials of the abbreviation, write out the word first, followed by the abbreviation in parentheses.

He is a graduate of the University of Rochester (UR).

Computer-integrated manufacturing (CIM) will be thoroughly investigated by our factory automation committee.

On the other hand, when the abbreviated form is more familiar than the written-out form, you should write the abbreviation first, followed by the spelled-out phrase in parentheses.

We have implemented SPC/SQC (statistical process control/statistical quality control) throughout our plant.

Semiconductors are primarily purchased by OEMs (original equipment manufacturers).

By defining every abbreviation at first use, you ensure that everyone understands it.

Occasionally, an abbreviation becomes so common that the abbreviated form is adopted as the standard form—for example, DNA and LSD. With these and similar abbreviations, the abbreviation (and not the word or phrase) should be used because it's more familiar to your reader. Some additional examples:

bc (blind copy)
CEO (chief executive officer)

CPA (certified public accountant)
DOD or DoD (Department of Defense)
DP (data processing)
EPA (Environmental Protection Agency)
ESOP (employee stock option plan)
FYI (for your information)
IBM (International Business Machines)
IRS (Internal Revenue Service)
MBA (master of business administration)
OEM (original equipment manufacturer)
OSHA (Occupational Safety and Health Administration)

Abbreviations that are growing in popularity but are not yet universally recognized and therefore should be spelled out the first time you use them include:

AP (accounts payable)
AR (accounts receivable)
CAD (computer-aided design)
CAE (computer-aided engineering)
CAM (computer-aided manufacturing)
CASE (computer-aided software engineering)
CIM (computer-integrated manufacturing)
CIO (chief information officer)
DBA (doing business as)
DTP (desktop publishing)
EDI (electronic data interchange)
GIGO (garbage in, garbage out)
IS (information systems)
LBO (leveraged buyout)
Mac (Macintosh personal computer)
OPM (other people's money)
PI (per inquiry)
QA (quality assurance)
QC (quality control)
RFP (request for proposal)
SOP (standard operating procedure)
SPC (statistical process control)
SQC (statistical quality control)

VAR (value-added reseller)
VDT (video display terminal)
WYSIWYG (what you see is what you get)

Note that the trend today is to omit internal and terminal punctuation in abbreviations: Thus, we write *RSVP* instead of *R.S.V.P.* Abbreviations without periods have a cleaner, more readable appearance.

The internal punctuation should be retained in proper names *(J. J. Jones)*, and the final period should be used when the abbreviation stands for a single word rather than a group of words. (Write *no.* to abbreviate the single word *number* but *UFO* to abbreviate the phrase *unidentified flying object.*)

Internal punctuation should also be retained when it is needed to eliminate any possible confusion. For example, medical doctor is abbreviated *M.D.* because *MD* is the abbreviation for Maryland. United States is abbreviated *U.S.* so that the reader does not think we are writing the word *us* in uppercase.

Rule 56. Do not use an apostrophe when writing the plural of an abbreviation.

The modern style is to omit the apostrophe when writing the plural of an abbreviation that does not contain periods. Although the abbreviation is in uppercase letters, the *s* should be lower case.

BLTs
OEMs
RFPs
UFOs

The apostrophe should also be omitted when referring to a decade.

the 1950s
the '90s

An apostrophe is used in the plural of an abbreviation that has a final period.

M.D.'s

Capitalization

Rule 57. Do not capitalize words to emphasize their importance.

The playwright William Wycherley once said, "Those who praise everyone do a vast disservice to those few who truly deserve it." In the same way, arbitrary capitalization of words to make them seem important or stand out can lead to confusion as well as cheapen those words that should be capitalized.

We offer a free Special Report on reducing computer costs to anyone who stops by our booth at PC Expo.	We offer a free special report on reducing computer costs to anyone who stops by our booth at PC Expo.
Our Company is now in its Fourth Year of continuous service to its many Customers in this country and abroad.	Our company is now in its fourth year of continuous service to its many customers in this country and abroad.
I pledge to give Value and Quality to all my clients.	I pledge to give value and quality to all my clients.

Capitalizing words to give them emphasis is old-fashioned and no longer in style. If you want to emphasize a word, underline it. Or set it in italic or boldface type. But again, don't overuse these techniques lest they lose their effectiveness.

Rule 58. Capitalize the full names of corporations, government agencies, divisions, departments, and organizations.

Official names and titles of business and government entities are capitalized.

U.S. Small Business Administration
J & R Medical Supplies, Inc.
Gralco Service and Support Division
Department of Defense

Do not capitalize words such as division, group, company, department, manufacturing, accounting, payroll, and quality control when they stand alone. They are capitalized only when they are part of an official name.

Take your pay stubs to Accounting and let them figure it out.	Take your pay stubs to accounting and let them figure it out.
He works in Quality Control.	He works in quality control.
I was formerly with the Westinghouse electronics and defense center in Baltimore, Maryland.	I was formerly with the Westinghouse Electronics & Defense Center in Baltimore, Maryland.
The Acme manufacturing company was, for many years, the largest employer in the county.	The Acme Manufacturing Company was, for many years, the largest employer in the county.
The Manufacturing Company closed down.	The manufacturing company closed down.

Titles are capitalized when they precede the person's name and usually are not capitalized when they follow the name. Therefore, you would write *President Harry Smith* but *Harry Smith, president of Westinghouse.*

Rule 59. Capitalize trade names.

When a trademarked product comes into general use, there's a tendency to confuse that trade name (e.g., Kleenex) with the thing itself (e.g., tissue).

In everyday conversation, we may well get away with using trade names loosely (saying, for instance, "Please Xerox this report" when it would be more accurate to say, "Please photocopy this report"). But when it comes to writing, you need to take special care to resist using trade names when you don't mean to use them. You do so to avoid blurring the distinction between a company-owned product and a generic term but also to avoid confusing the reader. Xerox is the name of one copier, not of the copying process; Kleenex is the name of one tissue; Kitty Litter is the name of one brand of cat-box filler.

To help you keep in mind the distinction between some trade names and their generic equivalents, we've listed some commonly encountered trade names on the left and the generic term on the right. Use the term on the left only when referring to that particular product; when referring generically to an item, use the term on the right. The trade names are capitalized; generic names are not.

Trade Name	*Generic Equivalent*
Astroturf	artificial grass
Band-Aid	adhesive strip, bandage
Coke, Coca-Cola	cola
Formica	laminated plastic
Jacuzzi	whirlpool bath
Jell-O	gelatin, gelatin dessert
Kitty Litter	cat litter, cat-box filler
Kleenex	facial tissue
Liquid Paper	correction fluid
Mace	chemical repellent
Magic Marker	marker, marking pen
Nautilus	exercise/weight machine
Novocaine	anesthetic, painkiller
Pampers	disposable diapers
Ping-Pong	table tennis
Q-Tip	cotton swab
Rolodex	rotating card file

Trade Name	*Generic Equivalent*
Sanka	decaffeinated coffee
Scotch Tape	clear tape, plastic tape
Sweet'n Low	artificial sweetener
Tabasco sauce	red pepper sauce
Valium	tranquilizer
Vaseline	petroleum jelly
Velcro	fabric fastener
Walkman	portable cassette player
Wite-Out	correction fluid
Xerox	copy, photocopy

Spelling

Rule 60. Know the basic rules of spelling.

Unlike the consistent, orderly punctuation rules, the rules of spelling are not always logical. The best spellers we know are the people who rigorously learn every word they catch themselves misspelling, not the ones who rely on rules.

Having said this, we'd like to give you the (abbreviated) rules, anyway. Aside from being a useful reference, they will help you understand the relationship between the rules and the types of misspellings that result from the exceptions to these rules.

I BEFORE E, EXCEPT AFTER C

In *ie* combinations, *i* almost always precedes *e*: niece, achieve. But use *ei* when the letters are preceded by *c* or when pronounced "ay": ceiling, receive; neighbor, weigh. (There are exceptions, such as *leisure, either,* and *weird.*)

Suffixes

A suffix is one or more letters or syllables added to the end of the word to change its meaning. The suffix in *grievance* is *-ance; -ly* is the suffix in *absolutely.*

Drop the final silent *e* before a suffix beginning with a vowel.

grieve	grievance
receive	receiving

Retain the final silent *e* before a suffix beginning with a consonant.

absolute	absolutely
care	carefully

Exceptions: true + *-ly* = truly; argue + *-ment* = argument; judge + *-ment* = judgment; acknowledge + *ment* = acknowledgment.

Double the final consonant before a suffix that begins with a vowel (like *-ing* or *-ed*) if one of the following conditions exists: (1) the word has only one syllable (like *cut* or *run*); (2) the word ends in a single consonant preceded by a single vowel and the accent is on the last syllable (like *rebel*).

sit	sitting
plan	planning
submit	submitted
regret	regrettable

If the accent of a two-syllable word is on the first syllable, do not double the final consonant before a suffix beginning with a vowel: cancel, canceled; travel, traveling.

In words ending in *-y,* change the final *y* to *i* if *y* is preceded by a consonant.

justify	justified
beauty	beautiful

Exception: if the suffix begins with *i,* retain the *y* before the suffix:

carry	carrying

"CEDE" WORDS

Except for *supersede, exceed, proceed,* and *succeed,* all words having the "cede" sound end in -*cede:* accede, precede, recede, concede.

PLURALS

To make a regular noun plural, add an *s.*

boy	boys
book	books

With irregular plurals, add *es* if the noun ends in *o* preceded by a consonant.

tomato	tomatoes
embargo	embargoes

Exceptions: piano, pianos; zero, zeros; solo, solos.

With nouns ending in *y,* change *y* to *i* and add *es* if the *y* is preceded by a consonant.

sky	skies
enemy	enemies

Add *s* if a noun ending in *y* is preceded by a vowel.

play	plays
day	days

Rule 61. If there are variant spellings, use the preferred one.

When a word may be spelled in more than one way, use the preferred spelling (i.e., the first spelling listed) in *Webster's Ninth New Collegiate Dictionary.*

acknowledgment, not acknowledgement
adviser, not advisor
benefited, not benefitted
canceled, not cancelled

catalog, not catalogue
dialogue, not dialog
judgment, not judgement
programmer, not programer
sizable, not sizeable
toward, not towards

Rule 62. Keep a list of the words you repeatedly misspell.

The spelling rules are helpful, but nothing is quite so helpful, especially to shaky spellers, as committing to memory those words they misspell frequently.

Since most people misspell only a small and predictable percentage of the words in the English language, it's not difficult to pinpoint the words that are most often misspelled.

For example, the majority of business writers misspell "supersede." People tend to put a "c" in place of the second "s." This isn't just coincidence; almost all words with that sound end in *-cede*. Also misspelled are these ten common words: judgment, canceled, accommodate, embarrassed, receive, occurred, beginning, guarantee, occasion, and develop.

By keeping a list of words you misspell, you'll be confronting most of the spelling problems you're likely to face on the job.

7

Principles of Format

In a society influenced by MTV, *USA Today,* desktop publishing, electronic mail, and video replays, written business communications must work harder than ever to catch—and keep—our readers' attention.

Never assume that the readers of your internal and external communications will be drawn to, and entranced by, a mere succession of paragraphs that strain the eyes and tax the brain.

A pleasing format helps your audience read what you've written. It is not enough to string ideas, sentences, paragraphs, and pages together coherently; the message must engage the eye as well as the mind. The format is the stage for your ideas, the store window that displays your mind's merchandise.

Attractive "packaging" means a clean and readable page with consistent spacing and margins in a letter or memo or a crisp, glossy presentation with subheads, illustrations, charts, and assorted typefaces in a formal proposal.

Wide margins make it easier for the eye to scan a page. A

concise yet specific "subject" or "Re" line helps encapsulate a memo and give the reader an overview of what follows.

This chapter details some ideas about planning the way your communications look—how to highlight your thoughts and smooth the path from the page to your reader's understanding, acceptance, and even enjoyment of your message.

For detailed guidelines on improving the look of print communications, read *Looking Good in Print*, 2nd ed., by Roger Parker (Chapel Hill, N.C.: Ventana, 1990).

Rule 63. Use wide margins to aid readability.

Architect Mies van der Rohe once summarized his feelings about architecture in a pithy statement that has been widely repeated: "Less is more."

The same idea is certainly true of words on a page. The wider the margins (up to a point), the more attention your message is likely to receive.

A dense page of type with narrow margins is difficult to read, not to mention off-putting to a busy person. The wider the line of type, the farther the eye has to jump to return to the left margin to begin a new line, and the easier it is to lose one's place while reading. Book designers are aware of this potential for eyestrain; that's why large-format books usually use two columns of type per page.

Make left margins at least an inch and right margins one-half to one inch. Leave at least one-inch margins on top and bottom, too. That way, your message will be neat and attractively framed on the page, command attention, and give your readers a type of visual breathing room that they will appreciate.

The rule of thumb is readability. Text should be at least one-quarter to one-half inch away from any graphic element on the page, such as rules, letterhead, address, charts, or bulleted lists.

Also, it's better to have wider margins and shorter paragraphs—and to spread a document over two pages to make it look airy and inviting—than to cram everything into long paragraphs in a misguided effort to stay within the confines of a one-page letter.

Rule 64. Use Subject or Re lines in memos.

"Subject" and "Re" lines help the reader identify a memo's topic and purpose quickly. They force the writer to identify the subject matter instead of forcing readers to piece it together for themselves.

For "Re" (for "regarding") and subject lines to be helpful, they should be specific, especially if your memo is one of many on the subject.

SUBJECT: Client Surveys	SUBJECT: Need for Improving Question 2 on Client Survey

The example on the right is specific. It not only tells the reader that the subject of the memo is the client survey; it answers the reader's question, What *about* the client survey?

You may use either a "Re" line or a subject line, but in either case it needs to be specific enough to embrace the main idea of the document. Here are a few more examples:

Re: Relocation Charges	Re: Relocation Charges for Kathy Byrne
Re: Performance Evaluations	Re: Forms for Performance Evaluations
Subject: Tristate Paper Clip Company	Subject: Clean-up Procedures at Tristate Paper Clip Company
Subject: Plant Payroll	Subject: Questions to Resolve Before Starting the Plant Payroll Project

Although being specific may involve a few more words, those words are well spent. A specific "Re" line or subject line gains the readers' attention by reminding them that you are writing about a subject of interest or are responding to their question or inquiry.

Re: ABC Company sales training seminars

Re: Your company's sales training needs

Re: Your company's upcoming sales-training seminar

Re: The information you requested on sales training for your sales force

Rule 65. Use modern salutations and closings in letters.

SALUTATIONS

There are several standard, acceptable salutations and closings in business letters. You can write:

Dear Mr. Jones:
Dear Ms. Jones:
Dear Bill,
Dear Lois,

Notice that you may use a comma instead of a colon when you are addressing your reader by first name. The problem is how to address someone whose name you don't know. The usual solutions lead to awkward, antiquated, or sexist phrases like "Dear Sir or Madam." (Can't you make up your mind?)

People in business sometimes resort to impersonal—and therefore ineffective—openings like "To Whom It May Concern" or "Dear Occupant," but these are cold clichés likely to be ignored.

What, then, do you do when you want to write to someone at an organization but you are unable or disinclined to find out the person's name? One solution is to address your letter generically. For example, you might address a complaint to a department store as "Dear Credit Manager" or "Dear Manager of Customer Relations." By using the title on the envelope and inside address of your letter, you are, at least, slotting the letter toward a particular department and, more specifically, to the head of that department.

A job seeker answering a blind ad (an advertisement that doesn't identify the name of a personnel person) may address the cover letter "Dear Advertiser," "Dear Potential Employer," "Dear Personnel Manager," "Dear Job Recruiter," or "Dear Reader."

A final note on salutations. Many people know their readers' names—but not their sex. For example, you may know that you want to write to Leslie Hawkings, Lee Arrons, and Terry Smith, but you are unable to determine if you are writing to a man or a woman. We suggest you use the person's full name—first and last— in the salutation. For example: "Dear Leslie Hawkings," "Dear Lee Arrons," and "Dear Terry Smith."

CLOSINGS

You may have come across many different ways of closing a letter around your office. Some are rather stiff: "Cordially," "Very truly yours," and "Respectfully." Even the popular "Sincerely yours," and "Yours truly" possess an antiquated feel.

The British use "Yours faithfully," which is a bit arch for American business writing; their less formal close is "Yours sincerely," which is still a mite formal.

Of the various possibilities, "Sincerely" seems the most neutral and versatile, followed by "Regards," which adds a dollop of friendliness to a business communication. The choice is yours. But steer away from the highly antiquated favorite of so many attorneys: "I remain." This is only a little better than the medieval "Your most humble and obedient servant."

Rule 66. Use numbered lists or bullets to present a series of points or ideas.

There are a variety of ways to format a message to make it more appealing to the eye and easier to read. Among these are bulleting and numbering. Let's look at the advantages of each.

BULLETING

When you have a list of parallel items in no particular sequence, bullet them for easier reading. Bullets (small solid circles at the start of a sentence or phrase) add drama to your writing, vary the rhythm of your message, and help you emphasize important points.

Paragraphs that do nothing more than provide a laundry list of miscellaneous facts are boring and repetitive; bullets let the reader focus instantly on what you're saying. They are also easier on the eyes.

When you list the benefits or drawbacks of something, for instance, use bullets to introduce each item. This new system

· eliminates all extra forms
· increases productivity
· reduces errors dramatically
· eliminates extra typing.

Notice that the bulleted items all start in verb form; this adds to the readability of the items. Be sure to maintain parallelism in any bulleted list.

NUMBERING

When you have items that follow one another sequentially, number them rather than putting them in paragraph form. This lets your readers follow the sequence more easily.

To open a new domestic correspondent account:

1. Submit a request to open an account to the managing director.
2. Wait for written approval.
3. Submit a copy of the approval to the accounts manager.

If there are more than fifteen or twenty items in your list, consider placing them in a table.

Rule 67. Put names in "cc" and "bc" lists in alphabetical order.

Following the closing of a letter or memo, you may list the names of people who will receive copies, introduced by "cc" (which stands for "carbon copy" or "courtesy copy") or "bc" (which stands for "blind copy"). A blind copy is one given to a third party without knowledge of others on the distribution list.

In some organizations, employees are asked to list the people on their "cc" list according to the hierarchy within the organization. Therefore, the CEO is listed first, regardless of whether the name is Zimbardo or Applebaum. The others follow according to their corporate rank.

The problem with this approach is that it may require time to think through the hierarchy of your readers. Also, if there are doubts as to the relationships, you may inadvertently alienate a manager by listing him or her in the wrong spot.

That's why, for the sake of convenience and speed, we suggest you alphabetize all cc and bc lists.

cc: Bob Aberdeen
     Betty Jones
     Tony Zimmer

Index

ABOUT THE AUTHORS

Robert W. Bly is director of The Center for Technical Communication (CTC), a company that specializes in improving the technical-writing skills of corporate employees and the quality of written communications within the organization. Mr. Bly holds a B.S. in engineering, has taught technical writing at the university level, and is the author of 25 books, including *The Copywriter's Handbook*. He was formerly a technical writer for Westinghouse Electric Corporation and also spent 10 years as a self-employed technical writer.

Gary Blake is director of The Communication Workshop, a consulting firm that presents on-site seminars on business writing, technical writing, and proposal writing. Among his clients are Hughes Aircraft, American Airlines, Lever Brothers, Symbol Technologies, Chase Manhattan Bank, and Van Den Bergh Foods.

Together Robert Bly and Gary Blake have written six books, including *The Elements of Business Writing*.

Readers wishing more information can reach the authors at the following addresses: Bob Bly, CTC, 174 Holland Avenue, New Milford, NJ 07646 (tel.: [201] 385-1220). Gary Blake, The Communication Workshop, 130 Shore Road, Suite 236, Port Washington, NY 11050 (tel.: [516] 767-9590).